Product Competitive
Intelligence

Product Competitive Intelligence

James Michael

Zelfin

Michael, James
Product Competitive Intelligence

ISBN 978-0-9997669-4-1

---

[1] https://creativecommons.org/licenses/by/4.0/deed.en_US

Contents

0

Introduction

Consumers have many choices when it comes to the products and services that they purchase. From the perspective of the consumer this would appear to be a nice problem to have, however in many instances it is difficult to discern which products offer the needed features at a fair value when there are many similar products on the market. Consumers are also motivated by selection criteria that are outside the scope of suitability to mission, price, and quality. They also look at environmental factors, whether the sources of raw materials were treated fairly in their acquisition, and whether the labor used to produce the goods was child or slave labor, or its equivalent. From a vendor point of view it is increasingly difficult to achieve distinction in a crowded market. There are a few success stories where careful marketing, a story that appeals to the target demographic, and a product that offers the consumer something more than its pure utility all come together. This book is about finding those distinctions in products, services, and systems which employ them, and using them to effectively market those products and services.

One of my first jobs after graduate school involved the development of a competitive intelligence system for a coatings business. Their primary marketing problem was the perception that their products were more expensive than the competing companies' products, which is a real problem when you are selling into a very cost conscious market. It was the realization of the power behind the system we developed that led to creation of this book. The world has changed in many ways since development of that system. People self-organize into smaller isolated groups. At the same time their reach and access is worldwide. Selection criteria has become sharper and more diverse.

The amount of data instantly in one's reach is staggering. In a few minutes it is possible to research possible products that might offer a solution to a problem, acquire a list of product choices, compare products, locate vendors who have the product in stock, find who offers it at the best price, and order it to be delivered the same day. There is therefore great value in accessing the consumer as early in that chain of events as possible. A purchase decision may be made anywhere along that chain. There are any number of triggers that might result in the purchase decision. Being in the chain provides a chance to be that trigger, which can be anything from a positive review to a comment regarding how environmentally responsible the manufacturer was with the packaging. Today the fact that you have manufactured a great product, provide an excellent warranty, and sell it at a competitive price is not sufficient to achieve the sales that are possible. You must build product awareness in a highly fragmented economy consisting of consumers with deeply held convictions.

As people self-organize into smaller and more restrictive demographics we may begin to identify the appearance of specific triggers associated within that demographic. This is readily apparent in the attention paid to packaging by those with serious concerns about the amount of plastic waste being produced. In years past there was a widespread belief that using recyclable plastics would alleviate much of the plastic pollution problem, however the crisis in plastic pollution in the oceans has shown that plastic being recyclable is only half the solution, the other being recycling actually occurring. When a large percentage of recyclable plastic is not recycled, then the amount of plastic pollution will continue to increase. For this reason those who are concerned about this issue take the amount of plastic packaging into account when selecting products. That is why plastic packaging can be a negative trigger for a product choice, i.e. a reason NOT to purchase.

Information is everywhere, but not much of it is useful without interpretation. A current fad is artificial intel-

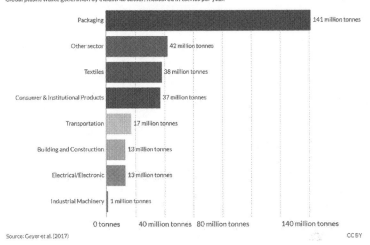

Fig. 1 - Plastic waste generation by industry

ligence or AI, which has been around a long time but advances in computing power are only now driving its adoption at scale. AI is used to derive relationships from correlations that are not intuitive using typical analytical techniques. One AI approach is the neural network. There are multiple variations on the idea, but the basic idea is to feed various data inputs in one end, adjust weighting factors during training that adjust the significance of each input, which is then fed into a nonlinear function that produces an output value. Training sets are used to adjust the weights so that the outputs match known or expected values. Once trained the neural net can operate on new data. Common uses are applications like pattern or image recognition.

For those who seek it data is available for nearly any purpose. It may be historical, current, highly targeted, or very general. That being said, accessing data that is useful for a specific purpose can be challenging and it is quite easy to be overwhelmed what is easily available. Search engine optimization has not helped matters and has turned common Web searching into an exercise in advertising avoidance. We need a more focused approach, one that starts with the product and then looks outward towards possible marketing targets, one that finds correlations between product attributes and drivers of purchase decisions by those targets. Consider the potential impact that a marketing methodology might have that takes into account competitive data on companies and their products, as well as the differentiating characteristics of concern to the micro-demographics that constitute the population of potential consumers. The potential increase in marketing effectiveness implies a need for a formal process to deliver targeted comparative information in a way that is most appealing to those specific market demographics. Marketing a product into a specific sub-market is better done from an understanding of the criteria important in that demographic. A systematic approach can be used that employs this outward looking methodology, that identifies a comprehensive set of dimensions, and then correlates those into criteria applicable to the demographics of interest. We can illustrate this through a simple example.

California leads the United States in environmental legislation. Appearing on many labels these days is a statement that gives many pause when considering purchase of a product - Determined to cause cancer in California. The phrasing generates the occasional "Good thing we're not in California" type of comment, but I mention it here because it is one of those little things that a consumer will note and take into consideration when making a decision whether to purchase a product. The State of California in effect places a negative trigger on such products. Consumers outside of California do pay attention and will often choose a different product when possible.

It is not possible to be all things to all consumers and address every single issue that someone might use as an objection to buying a product. The objective here is to provide a formal methodology for identifying those areas where a product may be shown to stand out among the competition within these micro-demographics so as to

16

build on the strengths of an existing product and at the same time, identify potential opportunities for future improvement.

The goal of this book is to develop the basis for Product Competitive Intelligence or PCI as an extension of, and complement to, Competitive Intelligence (CI) and Product Intelligence (PI), with the introduction of a third analytical tool, Micro-demographics Intelligence (MDI). We will explore the history and objectives of CI and PI, their advantages and disadvantages with respect to highly targeted product marketing. We will see that PCI is more than the intersection of CI, PI, and MDI since it includes elements of all as well as additional features resulting from their synergy.

In order to fully develop the concept of PCI we need to define what we mean by a product or service. We will also develop the concept of a system which incorporates two or more products or services.

The notion of properties and features is important in PCI so we will develop a methodology for documenting properties and features as metrics for comparison. Measurements permit objective comparisons, so long as the metric is consistent across competitors. To this end we will show how to normalize the units of measure (UOM) across the brands being compared. Through this process we will achieve a set of objective measurements, classifications, and other facts which can be put to use in establishing the superiority of a product based on a wide range of criteria.

Once we have established our superiority metrics we can begin construction of the value proposition that we can use as the trigger for a buying decision. Every decision criteria can be viewed as a potential trigger opportunity. Therefore many value propositions for a product may coexist.

To get to our value propositions we will need to determine the likely micro-demographics and their individual pain points or issues of concern. These concerns are cross-correlated with the comparative distinctions to find those which are global and local to the micro-demographics of interest. Knowing the scope of these distinctions permits a more accurate targeting of specific messages. For instance, members of PETA might be negatively triggered by the fact that a competing brand was tested on animals or positively triggered learning that your product contains no animal products and has never involved animals as test subjects. That message might be given low significance by the majority of other consumers. Conversely, as plastic pollution has become more noteworthy, a product's non-plastic packaging might have more global appeal and thus act as a positive trigger across multiple micro-demographics.

Ultimately your goal is to sell your products and services. Sometimes we must do so in the face of challenging facts. For instance, if your cost of production of a chemical cleaning agent is higher than the retail price of a competing brand then you need motivators beyond price. However, for the micro-demographic for whom price is an overriding concern this can be a very difficult sale. This is where context and system analysis can prove their worth. Although price might be a high value concern, it might be established that value in some other form might be shown to be more important. For instance, the amount of product needed to perform a task, the number of uses required, and similar metrics are used to educate the customer and overcome what on the surface appears to be a simple objection.

Systems of course will have similar normalization requirements as product properties and feature analysis, and we will show how to compare systems consistently between brands.

After getting the hang of the process, PCI becomes quite fun since one begins to note comparative features in all sorts of products and services, and realize the wide variety of positive and negative triggers that influence our buying decisions.

The use and benefits of PCI and its affiliated intelligence gathering methods are not limited to large organizations. Small companies are often more nimble and better equipped to make inroads into markets compared to a large company carrying baggage that interferes with the message being delivered. To illustrate this we will develop a case study around a small company servicing a local market for whom Amazon is a competitor.

Each chapter in this book has a set of exercises designed to help get you thinking about the ideas presented. There are no tests and no final exams, and there are no right or wrong answers to the exercises, but thinking about problems is the fastest route to solving them.

Exercise

1. List your objectives in reading this book.

2. For the objectives you listed, what are the metrics for success in determining whether you have achieved each objective?

3. What are some issues in public discourse around which you might create a marketing effort targeted at those who have strong convictions on the subject?

Competitive Intelligence

For as long as there has been competition there has been some form of competitive intelligence. The competitive landscape spans competitors, vendors, customers, industries, products, and markets. Competitive intelligence involves the acquisition of information associated with these entities, which is analyzed to develop effective business strategies. Competitive intelligence leverages information gained from all ethically available sources in pursuit of this goal.

As a formal approach competitive intelligence is said to have originated in the 1980s and is generally attributed to the publishing of Fuld's *Competitor Intelligence: How to Get it, How to Use it.*[1,2] The field has undergone much evolution and is now often referred to as Competitive Analysis.

Competitive intelligence has many potential benefits including the capability to know when new competitors are entering the market, discovering new trends and developments that may affect your products and services, as well as suggesting what your competitors may do based on your actions or due to other factors. Competitive intelligence may give you sufficient time to be proactive in dealing with such developments. Additionally, competitive intelligence can help you interpret the mistakes of your competitors so that you do not repeat them.

Competitive intelligence may be used at the macro or micro level in an organization in the development of business unit or corporate strategies. Multiple competitive intelligence techniques may be employed, including

1 https://www.imanet.org/-/media/58818383cf5b47a4a5229193b cdcb366.ashx

2 Fuld, Leonard M. - *Competitor Intelligence: How to Get it, How to Use it*, 1985

war games, win/loss analysis, technological disruption , and the preemptive analysis of changes that may affect the business including regulatory and environmental.[3]

Competitive Intelligence Centers

One approach to implementing competitive intelligence is the establishment of a Competitive Intelligence Center for your organization that will act as the hub for collection and distribution of competitive knowledge.

A key mission of your Competitive Intelligence Center is the review of your company's exposure to Competitive Intelligence efforts by your competition. Examine the potential attacks and threats which pose a risk. Establish procedures for sharing information with vendors and potential partners on projects. Many employees do not understand the requirements that may be associated with terms of non-disclosure agreements. Those terms often include a requirement that every disclosure of protected information be noted as such, whether communicated verbally or in writing. Employees may not realize how their social media activity might inform competitors of company activities, such as posting where they had lunch when dining with a customer on company business.

Information Warfare

Competitive Intelligence may involve elements of information warfare. Information from many sources may be used to form opinion and otherwise influence market behavior in some fashion.

Awareness of technological developments that affect the business is a critical part of the competitive intelligence effort, as is monitoring developments along regulatory fronts. International relations can play into long term business strategy and awareness of the impact that current events may have is critical. Political decisions can seriously impact markets, as recently observed with implementation of tariffs by the Trump administration.

---

3 https://www.fuld.com/methodologies/early-warning-detection-monitoring/

Gathering Information

There are many potential sources of information for your analysis. These include company websites, financial analysts who provide their opinion on the business operations of your competitors, industry analysts who look at the state of the industry and the companies that make it up, trade publications that provide information on the trends and hot topics of interest to those in your industry, web traffic analysis that may be used to discover trends in the public sphere, and social media that provides information of cultural trends and relative recognition of competitors by the trend setters and influencers.

Competitors vary in how they compete with your company. They may sell products and services very close to your own, or they may offer products and services that are different, but may be considered alternatives in some way. For instance, two manufacturers of chlorine for swimming pools may offer the chlorine in different forms, such as powder or tablets, but very similar products. While another competitor may sell an ozone treatment system. That competitor and the chlorine based product competitors both sell products that are used to sanitize water in swimming pools but the products are quite different.

Some competitors are more of a threat than others and deserve additional scrutiny. This may be governed by the rapidity of progress in your industry, the speed with which your competitor adopts and develops new products, and the time it takes for the impact of such developments to make it to the market.

Internal Sources

Each person in the company is potentially both a producer and consumer of competitive intelligence. Employees should be trained to observe and report information that might be relevant to the competitive intelligence effort as they interact with vendors and others in the industry. Competitive intelligence is used to build understanding of competitor strategy. By analyzing past competitor actions and monitoring competitor activities one may be able to predict the competitor's next moves.

One approach to experimenting with potential strategies is war gaming. Players assume the role of the companies in the game and compete to determine probable outcomes.

Much of the knowledge in an organization is held by the employees. Loss of employees can result in a loss of knowledge, as well as loss of contacts in the employee's network. A preemptive approach to retaining knowledge is to map this knowledge and identify where strategic gaps may occur in the event an employee leaves, maintain repositories of this knowledge as well as information about the networks. This can be facilitated as part of the program to include employees in the competitive intelligence effort. They are a source, not only to understanding external facts and events, but internal as well.

External Sources

Practitioners of competitive intelligence must know how to source information from internal and external sources. Although much information is available online, there are other sources that can be leveraged, and that includes individuals and organizations that can provide access to information not found elsewhere. It is important to broaden access to industry contacts. This might occur through cultivation of these sources at conferences, initiating contact through sources such as LinkedIn, and participating in professional groups and forums where they are active participants. Potential sources also include customers, contacts at trade shows, vendors, and other partners.

Risk Awareness

A key concept in competitive intelligence is being able to understand the potential impact of risks within the organization, not only how they impact your company, but how they might impact your competitors. These risks might span disaster scenarios to supply chain disruptions, and might point to strategic planning that puts your company well ahead of your competitor in the event the risk occurs. Many organizations fail to mitigate low probability high impact risks and place themselves in a "game over" state simply through lack of planning.

Some competitors place themselves at risk by not paying close attention to potential supply chain disruptions. Sudden and random imposition of tariffs by the United States in 2019 produced a lot of uncertainty for businesses whose planning was impacted. Would you want to build a $100 million plant when there is a risk that a significant amount of equipment going into it would be subject to a 20% tax?

Relationships

As machine learning and artificial intelligence make further inroads into business operations these techniques will increasingly be employed in competitive intelligence. However, they will never replace the value of cultivating relationships with vendors and others in your industry, and experts who provide valuable insight into the future developments that may affect your business.

Competitive intelligence permits you to better understand your competitors, their strengths and weaknesses, as well as their exposures. Be wary of the limitations as well. Companies can obfuscate or publish misleading information, particularly if they are aware that they are a target of your intelligence gathering efforts.

Analysis

Once intelligence is acquired it must be analyzed. One analysis approach is comparison of competitors' strengths, weaknesses, opportunities, and threats to one's own, commonly referred to as a SWOT Analysis. Strengths and weaknesses have many dimensions such as leadership, financial position, the segments of the market they occupy, the types of products they offer and their attributes, and their strategic positioning. Opportunities and threats arise from many potential sources and may be tied to technological change, consumer trends and sentiments, and external factors such as political developments. For instance, instability in an African nation that is a sole source of a competitor's raw material critical for a manufacturing process would be a potential threat to that competitor.

Action

Analysis of intelligence may suggest which approach you should take with respect to a competitor, whether to go after a market where your competitors are weak, develop completely new products or approaches to solving a problem, or competing with them head on.

Market Analysis

Aside from understanding your competitors, their strengths and weaknesses, competitive intelligence provides a better understanding of existing or new markets that may be under consideration, as well as formulation of strategies for entering the market, whether your strategy rests with cost or product differentiation, or with product focus. Analytical approaches vary depending on the type of data one has, the risks being analyzed, and the types of decisions being made. Example analytical approaches include the quantitative strategic planning matrix and Monte Carlo techniques.

Segmentation

Another key benefit of competitive intelligence is that is provides the ability to determine how the market may be segmented in order to address specific needs, target selected consumers, and position a brand with a value proposition that appeals to a particular set of consumers. Segmentation will come strongly into focus as we apply micro-demographics intelligence in the application of PCI. Think of segmentation in competitive intelligence as a macro level process and that within PCI is more at the micro level. At a macro level we might approach consumers on the basis of style, cost, or durability of products. We might market to consumers based on their income, occupation, or geographic location. Segments may be defined prior to analysis, or may be an outcome of our analysis and arrived at heuristically.

Market segments will be viewed in terms of their potential, thereby targeting those for which the expected return on the marketing effort will be highest. Whether you sell your products and services directly to consumers, via online sales, or through retail channels, the segment must be one that you can access with your message and which will elicit sales from your efforts. A consumer who loves your products but can't afford them isn't your customer.

Case Study: Sparkling Pools

Let's examine an example competitive intelligence operation for a swimming pool company, Sparkling Pools. Sparkling Pools is a swimming pool installer and maintenance company that sells a complete line of pool chemistry and equipment. They manufacture their own line of pool chemicals under their brand. Since they provide maintenance services they sell their products as part of the maintenance. They compete with Amazon and local vendors for chemical and equipment sales. They compete with freelancers and other pool maintenance businesses in the area for services. Amazon may be making inroads on their service business through their service offerings.

In order to better understand their competitive position Sparkling Pools decides to implement a competitive intelligence department within the company and the employees are given the responsibility to make the effort a success. The employees are trained on their responsibilities in maintaining company confidentiality as well as information gathering techniques. Their network of contacts is cataloged and they are given competitive intelligence assignments. Through their competitive intelligence efforts they have determined that none of the local competitors make their own chemicals. They also learn the types of customers that their competitors are serving as well as the approximate volume of sales.

Pool maintenance is a highly competitive business. There has been negative price pressure in the maintenance business and their maintenance sales have been declining for 2 years. They are trying to decide whether to remain in the maintenance business or make changes in the way they run the business.

The competitive intelligence group at Sparkling Pools decides to research the logistics of pool maintenance to see if their business can be made more efficient. Using GIS data and public records of permits, they are able to plot the location of permitted pools and spas in the market area. They create maintenance routes based on this data and focus their marketing efforts on the pool owners in close proximity to the routes, leaving the widely separate pools and spas to competitors, thereby decreasing their efficiency. Next, they initiate a plan to recruit the freelancers in the area to sell their maintenance products by offering them at a compelling discount. They research the possibility of offering a Certified Maintenance Technician program for training the freelance pool maintenance technicians in the use of their pool maintenance system. The certification program offers a new revenue stream, builds trust in the brand, and instills confidence in customers that their pool is being properly maintained when they hire a certified technician. This will lead to additional sales of the Sparkling Pools brand supplies as the freelancers promote the brand to their customers. The relationship with the freelancers also provides an additional source of competitive information as well as a ready supply of employee candidates when members of the employee maintenance crews decide to move on.

Exercise

1. Referring to the Example , how might Sparkling Pools begin to differentiate itself in its market?

2. Do you think Sparkling Pools can dominate its market? What do you think market domination would mean for Sparkling Pools?

3. How might Sparkling Pools learn about new competitors in its market?

4. How might Sparkling Pools determine whether they should stay in the maintenance business? What would be a good strategy if they decided to leave the maintenance business?

2

Product Intelligence

Product Intelligence (PI) has evolved since the field was introduced in 2002 by Averna Technologies to describe a process to help test engineers develop test automation systems. Further refinement by Averna occurred in 2009 and 2011 with the addition of automated versioning, configuration management, and quality enforcement.[1]

Current Practice

Siemens expanded the concept of PI with its Mind-Sphere system which finds insights in contextualized product performance data. Siemen's interpretation of PI utilizes data from product lifecycle management, enterprise resource planning, manufacturing execution systems, quality management systems, customer relationship management, Internet of Things (IoT) and other enterprise data for analytics which creates context by classifying and linking product-related attributes.[2]

Current approaches are integrating additional data sources such as social media to discover opportunities to improve products as well as to create new ones. Product differentiation, geographic based product preferences, and similar insights can be derived through the use of both structured and unstructured data.[3]

Ipsos released a PI offering in 2018 which enables marketers to evaluate products more quickly versus traditional product testing. The system utilizes online user ratings and reviews, gathers consumer feedback on products

1 https://en.wikipedia.org/wiki/Product_intelligence

2 https://www.plm.automation.siemens.com/global/en/products/performance-analytics/product-intelligence.html

3 https://datafloq.com/read/advantages-product-intelligence-company/12

in the market, and analyzes social data. Text analytics, bolstered by human intelligence, provide in-depth product performance insights based on unfiltered consumer feedback. This approach permits marketers to learn which product features drive satisfaction, gain an understanding of their product's strengths and weaknesses, and uncover how their product performs versus real-world competition.[4]

Artificial intelligence is becoming increasingly important in the field of Product Intelligence. Cognizant has developed a system which improves retail product metadata through the use of AI.[5]

The term Product Intelligence is now starting to appear in reference to "intelligent products" which might be autonomous in some fashion or have capabilities to communicate or interact with other products. In our usage, we only refer to PI in the sense of analysis of products, use of products, and product design, and not in reference to intelligent products.

Potential Areas of Growth

The field of Product Intelligence has been increasing in scope since its inception. In one sense this may be due to software vendors developing analytical approaches for which they need to apply a classification, for which PI is a good fit. In another sense this is a fledgling field which has much room to expand. It's quite possible that the scope of PI may increase quite significantly into what we are defining as Product Competitive Intelligence, however a key differentiator with PCI is the inclusion of Competitive intelligence as part of its core. It's a fuzzy world with a lot of overlap, and therefore plenty of room to choose tools and methodologies that accomplish the mission, regardless of how they may be categorized.

---

4 https://www.ipsos.com/en-ch/ipsos-launches-product-intelligence

5 https://www.cognizant.com/whitepapers/using-ai-to-enhance-the-quality-of-retail-product-metadata-codex3263.pdf

Datahut has defined Product Intelligence as deep understanding, insights and analytics on a company's products and that of its competitors, and how both are merchandised and sold in the marketplace.[6] That's a pretty good definition and one that we will adopt in this book since it leaves plenty of room for interpretation.

PI and PCI Differentiation

A key to understanding PI in the context of PCI is that the focus of PI is at the product level, whereas PCI tries to take a more holistic approach with respect to competition and expansion of its scope well beyond products. For many, PI may be sufficient to provide understanding, competitive advantages, and insight into how products might be improved.

Data Acquisition

Techniques of PI vary with the scope associated with the various software implementations. However we can generalize the approach to encompass the best of these different methodologies as they apply to PCI. Our need for PI is in the acquisition of product data for one's own and competitor data, social media content, reviews, consumer comments, and other information that provides insight into customer needs and issues as they pertain to the products. There are many discrete sources of product data such as labels, brochures, manufacturer websites, reviews, public filings, social media, and Internet news groups and forums.

Labels

Product labels are provide a treasure trove of competitor data. The data includes the amount of product by weight, volume, or quantity; ingredients, usually in order of amount; instructions for use; cautions and restrictions on use, often with reference to other safety data to

---

6 https://blog.datahut.co/how-to-use-product-intelligence-to-win-customers/

be found elsewhere. Accessing and exporting label data can be quite challenging. In some cases the manufacturer might provide label data online. Some label data can be found in government databases, such as that of pesticides. Vendors selling products online may provide product images that include label data. In many cases the manner in which the data is acquired is by fieldwork or purchase of the product.

When copying or exporting label data be sure to include it all. Details from instructions for use of a product can prove highly useful in comparisons.

Regardless of the location of the label data, in most cases that data may be impossible to acquire in an automated fashion due to the variation in formats between manufacturers. Databases would be the most useful provided they contain current data. Due to the amount of error correction that might be involved, scanning and OCR are probably not the ideal approach to data gathering when labels are involved.

Brochures

Brochures may contain much more detailed data on products. A common format for electronic versions of brochures is PDF. Although this may make access easier, consistent extraction of the data contained in brochures may prove as challenging as data extraction from labels. OCR and similar tools may be helpful, however the need to correct output from such tools can make it preferable to use a data entry person for data extraction operations. Robotic Process Automation or RPA is a product suite from UIPath that includes automation capability including data extraction from PDF files.[7]

Manufacturer Websites

In some cases the same data that is published in brochures is also published on the company website. This

---

7 https://www.uipath.com/rpa/robotic-process-automation

data is much easier to extract. Screen scraping or web scraping refers to extraction of data from websites by parsing the data from the HTML encoded pages. Scripts written in programming languages such as Perl and Python can quickly process such pages.

Reviews

It is human nature to complain. Reviews provide consumers an opportunity to air their grievances about all aspects of the products they purchase. Given the tendency of people to be more inclined to complain than to praise, it's understandable that there may be a large number of negative reviews even for non-defective well designed products. Mistakes happen and things get damaged. Sometimes a bad unit gets through quality control. However, in terms of data, information in reviews can be very useful. Poor performance, badly written instructions, failure to successfully implement new features, addition of unwanted features, and similar knowledge is there to be analyzed and used as input into new product ideas. In some cases complaints produce insight into important issues not detected in the quality control process. For instance a bad run of components may not be detected until the units start failing in the field. An early warning will be people complaining of failures.

Depending on the product and the sales numbers it may or may not be challenging to acquire data from reviews. Text analysis using approaches like word counts may be useful in discovering issues and trends associated with products.

Public Filings

There are numerous sources of public filing data for products, in particular products subject to special regulation such as pesticides. Corporate plans may be telegraphed via patent and trademark filings. Success of the company's divisions may be seen in some securities filings and other public reports.

Social Media

The selfie generation is eager to share their use of products and also tend to self-aggregate in groups that have unique demographics. Although we will delve into this in more detail in future chapters, social media is your place to learn about the trends and issues that hold sway among various interest groups. There are many different social media platforms. Many of them publish an API that offers the capability for your team to extract data from streams produced on the platforms. Key word searches, word proximity, word counts, and similar text analysis approaches can help in your research to find the chief motivators and demotivators for consumers of your products.

Internet News Groups and Forums

News groups and forums were the precursors to social media. They have declined somewhat in popularity, and they are usually not product-specific, but can be of great value for future product research and development. Public commentary regarding unmet needs as they relate to the intended use of a manufacturer's products might be discerned through the analysis of news group feeds. For instance, a hair products manufacturer might make what they believe is a comprehensive line of products, and then find that there is a need for a product that addresses a specific issue within a cultural and location based demographic.

Case Study: Sparkling Pools

As part of their strategy to position the Sparkling Pools brand of pool chemicals, the competitive intelligence group at Sparkling Pools begins a comprehensive analysis of the chemicals on the market that are sold locally and on Amazon. They catalog every chemical, obtain the safety data sheets and other documentation to learn as much as they can about the composition of the competing products. They also begin researching consumer sentiment regarding pool chemicals to learn more about customer likes and dislikes regarding pool products, complaints about products and vendors, and also try to discover issues that are not resolved by currently available products. One common complaint is chlorine and its effects such as making hair turn green, the smell, irritation, and allergic reactions. Sparkling Pools decides to develop a new chlorine free anti-bacterial treatment for pools and spas. There are competing chlorine-free products which Sparkling Pools must market against. The competitive intelligence group decides to take a comprehensive look at its chemistry lineup to arrive at a product strategy that will position their brand as the premium choice for pool and spa chemistry.

Exercise

1. Choose a company to research and find all patents filed by the company in the past year. What product innovation do you think has occurred within this company?

2. What complaints do people have with the company you researched in 1?

3. List some products made by the company. Find reviews associated with these products. What problems has the company had with the products? What have they done about them?

3

Micro-demographics Intelligence

The Internet and expansion in global communications and travel has facilitated dramatic shifts in culture. The increase in connectedness has made it easier to self-aggregate around special interests. At the same time the technological progress has also contributed to serious global issues which have resulted in further societal segmentation. This has a number of effects for those attempting to reach the consumers in these groups. Micro-demographics intelligence can be used to analyze these aggregations to determine the dimensions of interest most likely to be influential in purchasing decisions as well as vectors of communications for delivery of information of interest. Micro-demographics Intelligence is the third critical component in Product Competitive Intelligence.

The Global Community

It seems only a few short years since Arpanet led to the network of networks that eventually became the Internet. The real explosion occurred in the 1990s when the commercial potential of the Internet began to be realized and the new communication medium was seen as the solution to nearly every problem. In many respects these visions were accurate. The Internet has accelerated the pace of change in many fields including medicine, science, and engineering. Vast fortunes have been created in the process.

The networks that form the Internet, satellite communications, and other technologies have all contributed to the increased ease of global communications. Text messaging and cellular technology facilitate easy global communication. Emerging 5G technology, supplemented by technologies such as IoT and Blockchain will expand this trend even further.

The Self-Aggregation Effect

The early visionaries saw the Internet as a great equalizer providing everyone with access to information. However, an interesting side effect has occurred. The ease with which people can now communicate increased the ability of people to find others of similar interests, and this effect has not been limited to Internet dating. On the contrary, the effect on global culture has been a trend toward self-aggregation around areas of interest. As groups congregate around their self-interests they are more susceptible to the influence of their compatriots as they reinforce each other's viewpoints. Thus viewpoints within these groups may become sharper as they are not tempered by others outside the group. Members of these groups are thus more susceptible to the influence of memes through exposure and repetition. This self-aggregation effect is much akin to the cultural differentiation noted by anthropologists which occurs when a population is suddenly separated by a barrier.

Impact of World Events

The increase in global awareness has led to increased visibility of events on the world stage. People become more aware of injustices that have been perpetrated and may have access to first hand accounts of such events. Awareness of the global impacts of pollution and greenhouse gases lead to further self-aggregation around these concerns. Group-think that is politically motivated may lead to the growth and proliferation of extremist philosophy and may facilitate the rise of authoritarianism, while less extremist viewpoints may still be associated with an increase in nationalism and resulting economic impacts such as protectionist policies like tariffs. This may lead to a great deal of uncertainty for consumers and producers alike.

Self-Aggregation and Information Delivery

The effects of self-aggregation extend to communication and exposure to news and other information as those in similarly motivated groups may cluster in ways that limit access and delivery of information. For instance, those in groups very tightly aligned with environmental concerns may tend to receive news and communications from only a very restricted set of sources. This makes general marketing less effective. However, it also increases the opportunity for highly targeted marketing using the many social media channels that may be available. It may thus be easier to market highly focused products at a lower cost. Products having more general appeal may leverage marketing focused on the interests of the members of these groups.

Vectors of Communication

There are a number of effective vectors of communication to and within these micro-demographics including memes, news, rumors, word of mouth, influencers, and thought leaders.

Micro-demographic Dimensions

Micro-demographics may have many dimensions, including interests, values, purpose, beliefs, locale, profession, and membership.

Gathering Micro-demographic Intelligence

We can clearly see that there many potential avenues of research in the areas of micro-demographics that may yield useful information for targeting those groups that may form potential markets for a product or service. The challenge is in acquiring what might be classified as actionable intelligence, i.e. the information that is useful in determining what message would be of interest and to which populations. That information is at the core of why these micro-demographics exist, provided our thesis is correct. If self-aggregation occurs and the Internet is a key facilitator of that self-aggregation, then the key data we seek should be found on the Internet. More specifically, it should be found where the self-aggregating groups communicate, where they acquire news, and where they spend time. Since Internet communication is largely text based, text analysis should be a key component of intelligence gathering.

Text Mining

Text mining, or text analytics, may be used to retrieve text content, analyze it, and derive relationships that are not readily apparent via the usual modes of Internet searches and reading. Text mining is a software-centric approach employing scripting tools such as Python, Perl, and R.

There are many and varied sources of text for analysis and this may present one of the most interesting challenges in the intelligence gathering process. The starting point might be the product or service being offered. Who are the likely customers? Do they belong to a restricted set like swimming pool owners? Are they restricted to a particular locale such as homeowners in Atlanta Metro? Dimensional analysis of the product or service being sold will reveal additional jumping off points for text retrieval and mining.

General news feeds in which the public posts comments are a rich source of information on the culture and what are considered important issues. Mining these sources using word frequency analysis may turn up insights that might escape unnoticed by most people. For instance, interest in a new technology that has a potential impact on sales of your products might be measured over time. As that interest grows the potential risk to sales may also increase.

Consumer Dimensions

Companies usually have a pretty good idea who their customers are likely to be. If they sell cameras they can expect to sell a portion to photo hobbyists, a few to professional photographers, and some to those going on vacation. Each of those groups tend to have needs specific to the type of photography they intend to do, however those needs will vary within each subset. Professional sports photographers have different needs than professional portrait photographers. Understanding these dimensions may lead us to additional differentiating dimensionality. A nature photographer may have a higher inclination to be strongly motivated by environmental concerns than the sports photographer.

As we explore these consumer dimensions we will discover that special interests and professional affiliations have associated aggregation points on the Internet. Photography forums may be dedicated to a single special interest such as wildlife photography. Another may be associated with professional portrait photographers. Travelers frequent travel related sites.

Making Intelligence Useful

Mountains of data are useless without context and meaning. Acquiring actionable intelligence implies putting the information we gather and the analytical results into a form which is usable in the overall intelligence effort. Categories, classifications, summations, and aggregations permit cross-comparison across search areas. Continuing with the photography example, suppose we have uncovered 20 potential sources of text for analysis, all representing Internet photography forums across different interest subareas. We might examine word frequencies on a month by month basis for the past year for each of these sources. What are the correlations with other sources? What trends exist? Are there trends that span sources or do they tend to be localized? Are there obvious memes being promulgated and if so does the activity span aggregation points?

Consumers being multidimensional we expect to encounter reasons outside a product's fitness for use as a factor in a purchase decision. Understanding these dimensions is part of micro-demographics intelligence. Exploring these dimensions to gain insight into these motivating factors is key. The dimensions of a product extend beyond the product's intended use, but also to its source, the labor required in its manufacture, the raw materials, packaging, and even the fairness of the company in dealing with its suppliers. Micro-demographics intelligence represents a powerful approach to understanding consumers, their motivations, the factors that they may consider in making a purchase decision, and the degree to which those factors constitute overriding criteria in that decision.

Case Study: Sparkling Pools

The competitive intelligence team at Sparkling Pools has been assigned to acquire micro-demographics intelligence on all likely consumers of its products and services. They divide the consumers into local and online, and the sales into products and services. During this initial analysis they note that they provide no online services, and tag that as an area of research for the Product Intelligence group since there might be an opportunity to develop an online pool maintenance app or something similar. They end up with three primary areas to focus their micro-demographics research:

- Local Products
- Online Products
- Local Services

They begin accumulating intelligence relevant to these products and services by searching and analyzing text from news groups associated with pool owners, those with medical issues where pools, spas, or hot tubs are mentioned, local discussion groups, product reviews, and consumer complaints. They also perform text analysis on general discussion topics and word frequency on Twitter. Global warming and plastic pollution are high frequency topics. These facts are noted for further competitive and product intelligence analysis to determine what the relative carbon footprint and plastic pollution associated with each competitor might be in relation to Sparkling Pools.

Sparkling Pools' maintenance technicians drive gasoline powered vans. The competitive intelligence team decides to investigate the possibility of using electric vehicles both as a cost saving measure and as an aid in establishing the company as a carbon neutral enterprise.

Through its intelligence gathering the team learns that water sports are very popular in the area and there are many who participate who do not own a pool. This includes members of swim teams and water polo teams. There are few sources of the equipment needed by these participants in the local market, and that is a frequent topic of discussion for participants. They refer this observation to the Product Intelligence team for potential expansion of the product line.

Exercise

1. For a product or service, list its likely consumers.

2. What memberships might the consumers in 1 fall into?

3. Find as many special interests groups who would have members who are likely to be consumers of the product or service in 1.

4

Product Competitive Intelligence

Product Competitive Intelligence is a holistic merger of Competitive Intelligence, Product Intelligence, and Micro-demographics Intelligence.

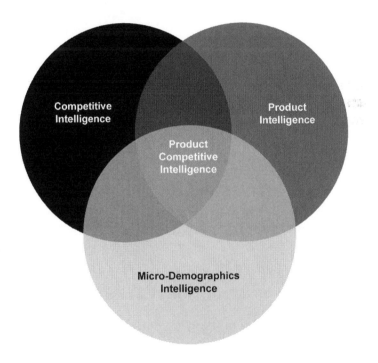

Fig. 1 Product Competitive Intelligence incorporates features of Competitive Intelligence, Product Intelligence, and Micro-Demographics Intelligence

Product Competitive Intelligence Approach

There are several points that are key to understanding Product Competitive Intelligence. Competitive Intelligence provides insights into competitor capabilities, strategies, strengths, and weaknesses. Products and services have physical attributes, features of use, benefits, and other metrics that can be used to compare and contrast similar products and services across manufacturers. Consumers of products and services have a range of interests, concerns, pain points, and other metrics which can be viewed in the context of product selection and use. By applying differentiation between products in the context of specific user criteria we can position a product as superior where the distinction will be considered relevant. Not all consumers are interested in the same criteria, so we want to focus these criteria based distinctions or filters where they will be most effective.

Applying Product Competitive Intelligence

There are several steps to effective utilization of Product Competitive Intelligence. The first step is determination of the dimensions of comparison that will be employed. This may be done in coordination with analysis of micro-demographics that constitute the target markets. Here we will determine which properties and features of your products to compare in order to establish why your product is superior to your competitors. We next develop targeting strategies to bring awareness of the benefits your products and services have with respect to issues and concerns of importance.

Product Competitive Intelligence overcomes the limitations of Competitive Intelligence and Product Intelligence by merging both approaches and then extending both through the use of Micro-demographics Intelligence.

Strategy

Strategic use of Product Competitive Intelligence involves identifying the comparative dimensions that matter most to the micro-demographics being targeted. Determine the key pain points, concerns, or other triggers for these micro-demographics in order to determine how differentiation of your product can leverage these triggers. There are many potential dimensions of comparison such as time, cost, lifetime, suitability to use, sustainability and environmental impact. Concerns of target demographics may be shared, therefore examine target demographics and then look at ways to group and segment.

Terminology

Attribute - a property associated with a product or service. Attributes are descriptive and often common across competing products. Paint has an attribute *coverage* representing the amount of surface that could be covered per unit of paint. A pool chemical may have an attribute that specifies the amount to use per 1,000 gallons of water. The attribute may have a contingency. For instance the pool chemical quantity might depend on the degree of turbidity of the water being treated.

Benefit - a property, result, advantage or other consequence of using a product or service that is generally considered positive. For instance, a benefit of the over the counter medication ibuprofen is that is alleviates pain. The benefit of an algaecide in a swimming pool is that it prevents algae from growing in the pool.

CI or **Competitive Intelligence** - The acquisition and analysis of data pertaining to competing companies to determine their capabilities, risk exposures, strengths, and weaknesses that may be employed to guide a company's strategic planning.

Comparison - In Product Competitive Intelligence a comparison is the process of documenting the properties, features, benefits and other factors across competing products in a consistent manner to facilitate the determination of competitive advantages of one product or service over another, particularly in the context of criteria important to members of target markets and demographics.

Feature - Generally, a property of a product or service or a by-product of its use. Often a feature is a distinguishing characteristic unique to one of a set of competing products, such as environmentally friendly packaging.

Micro-demographic - A population having distinguishable interests, mores, values, or other characteristics that give rise to triggers. A micro-demographic is often the result of Internet based self-aggregation around a distinguishing interest or belief.

PCI or **Product Competitive Intelligence** - The process of analyzing the properties, features, benefits, disadvantages, and other factors relating to competing products and services, and the identification of factors useful in establishing the superiority of a product or service based on criteria important to identified market segments associated with a micro-demographic.

PI or **Product Intelligence** - Deep understanding, insights and analytics of a company's products and services and those of its competitors, and how both are merchandised and sold in the marketplace

System - Within the context of Product Competitive Intelligence , a system is a combination of products and/or services which are used together to achieve an end goal. A pool treatment system might consist of a set of complementary products which keep the water sanitary, clear, and free of algae. System comparisons may illustrate superiority over a competitor when product by product comparisons fail to do so. For instance, individual products may be priced higher than the competition while the system results in higher productivity and greater profit.

Trigger - In Product Competitive Intelligence a trigger is a fact, distinction, or other criterion that may positively or negatively influence a purchase decision. A trigger may be, and often is, specific to a micro-demographic and associated with a value proposition. For instance, a product may have been tested on animals which could be a trigger for animal rights advocates. A product may use sustainable packaging that might appeal to those with environmental concerns.

UOM or Unit of Measure - Products and services are usually sold in some type of unit. For products this is often the package size, but it may be termed something other than a measure of weight or volume, such as use. Milk is usually packaged in the USA in quart, half-gallon, and gallon sizes. Other countries may use liters or other metric measures. Pool chemicals might be sold by the pound or kilogram, or by the liter, quart, or gallon. Dry products tend to be sold by weight whereas liquid products tend to be sold by volume. There are also specialty units of measure such as the cord for a quantity of firewood. Services might be priced by the hour or by some metric of work performed. A house painter might charge by the number of square feet of paint surface. A carpet cleaner might charge by the room. In order to compare products and services among vendors it is important to use an equivalent UOM in the comparison. The process of converting competing products to a consistent unit of measure is called normalization.

Value Proposition - The positioning of a product or service to establish a trigger based on one or more comparison metrics and values characteristic of a micro-demographic.

PCI Methodology

Product Competitive Intelligence is a multi-step process that leverages knowledge of competitor products, interests and concerns of consumers, and company competitive intelligence in the design and marketing of products. Product Competitive Intelligence might be applied to an existing product to assess its competitiveness such as in preparation for a marketing effort.

The methodology can be broken down at a high level into the following specialties:

- Competitive intelligence
- Product intelligence
- Micro-demographic intelligence
- Product feature analysis
- Positioning strategy
- Targeted marketing

Competitive Intelligence in PCI

Competitive intelligence is employed to determine the strengths and weaknesses of competing companies, particularly as those may apply to determination of triggers sensitive to specific micro-demographics. Understanding a competitor's processes and products may yield strategies for leveraging the differentiators that help you build your value proposition. A pool chemical company may decide to go totally plastic free in its chemical packaging and use that to distinguish itself to those for whom plastic pollution is a concern.

Memetics

In current parlance meme often refers to a short video or gif animation excerpted from popular culture that is used to express humor over a situation. More generally, and how we use the term, meme refers to an idea that takes hold and spreads within a population like a virus. Memetics is the study and use of memes, which is particularly effective as a marketing tool. Apple was extremely effective in meme building for its early products such as the iPod and iPhone. Limited availability was used to drive a sense of superiority for those who were able to acquire newly released products. Long lines of people camping outside stores overnight were shown on the news. This was very well orchestrated. Never discount the power and reach of those with access and influence over popular culture, they should be a part of your marketing team.

Product Intelligence

Products are created, evolve, go in and out of fashion, and sometimes disappear. They may disappear due to failure to evolve, or because external forces force them to. The introduction of the automobile did not help the buggy whip industry. How might the buggy whip industry have evolved and survived in the wake of transportation progress has been the subject of debate. However, it does illustrate a key point about products and their lifecycles. Those who produce products and provide services should avoid the myopia that makes them oblivious to sea changes in culture, technology, and other macro influences on the consumer. Moore's Law has led to massive increases in data capacity and throughput leading to rapid evolution in storage technology which continues apace today. Product intelligence can provide insight into these changes at an early stage, providing an organization time to modify its strategy to accommodate change. It also provides insight into competitor innovation capacity. Under certain circumstances, for instance where product evolution is constrained by known physical or technological limitations, the bounds on such innovation may be predicted with reasonable certainty.

Micro-demographics Intelligence

An important aspect of Product Competitive Intelligence is gaining an understanding of the members of the micro-demographics constituting your target market. There is always overlap in that members of one group may be members of another and thus may be more generally targeted. There are many ways to approach micro-demographics, but it is essentially a matter of applying dimensional analysis to popular culture and then finding groupings based on that analysis. Keyword analysis in social media, press coverage of issues and analysis of the influencers commenting on the issues, analysis of industry trends, all are valid approaches to identifying dimensions of interest. The micro in micro-demographics can mean just that - tiny. Some products target a very small consumer base, such as Linux systems administrators. What triggers might be of interest to this group? In their public discussions are there technology debates that reach the level of religious fervor? Does your product offer a trigger to those in the debate? Who is an influencer within that space? What strategies might you use to gain that influencer's trust and recommendation? Not all influencer marketing is bought and paid for. It might simply arise from asking for advice and input. For instance, you want to position your product favorably to members of PETA. You think you have done a good job of identifying all of the potential negative triggers to PETA members. Why not ask an influencer in that space for advice and confirmation? You might be surprised that you missed an important trigger point.

Analyzing Product Features

Product feature analysis involves identification of the dimensions of your product from the perspectives of the relevant demographic-specific trigger points you have identified. That includes the simple features such as cost per use. To address more complex triggers such as ecological impact, derivative statistics might be useful. For example, your packaging contains 3 grams of plastic, all recyclable. Your competitor's packaging contains 12 grams of recyclable and 24 grams of non-recyclable plastic. Those statistics are not as compelling as they might be if you calculate and compare the annual use of each product. This might be especially useful if the number of uses of the competing product is less than your product, thereby amplifying the comparison and strength of the trigger. An ounce of pollution per package might not carry the same impact as a trigger that several pounds per year would have.

Positioning Strategy

Knowledge of likely positive and negative triggers, product dimensions and attributes, competitive intelligence findings, and comparative product information provides inputs into the positioning strategy. Is your product the cheapest, fastest, most productive, easiest to use, or most environmentally friendly? Which negative triggers apply to your competition? Which apply to your product? How can you overcome potential negative triggers?

Sustainability is a sort of all-encompassing term that encapsulates many environmental concerns. Let's look at how a sustainability approach can be used to mitigate negative environmental triggers in your products. Suppose you manufacture a product that has a negative environmental impact but is needed to perform a critical business function. For instance it might be an anti-corrosion formulation. Next suppose that the chemical characteristics make it impossible to ship in anything other than a non-recyclable plastic container. How do you position this product in a way that minimizes the associated negative triggers? Even though consumers of that specific product may not be susceptible to the triggers, purchasers of other products you manufacture may look at your entire company's corporate responsibility as it comes to the environment. That is your key to overcoming this type of trigger. Through the purchase of carbon credits, contributing to plastic pollution cleanup efforts, and similar actions, you can position your company as sustainable with a neutral carbon footprint and net negative plastic pollution score.

Positioning strategy varies with our target micro-demographics. Some advantages are of interest to all and some are only of interest to the specific demographic. One way to think of this is a hierarchy, where the universal aspects are at the root and highly specific ones are in lower categories.

Targeted Marketing

Once the positioning strategy is known the next step is marketing to the specific recipients of the marketing campaign - the micro-demographics of interest. Marketing can take many forms and is driven by the characteristics of the micro-demographic in question. It may range from the wording on packaging to information delivered via social media and targeted ads.

Targeted marketing is an opportunity to think outside the box in search of new ways to reach those in highly specific niches. As per the earlier example where the product is targeted at a small user base, achieving buy-in from those in the community can go a long way toward creating a market for a product. A great example of this was Red Camera. They developed video cameras featuring large sensors that were desired by the amateur filmmakers of the day. They carefully fed news about what they were working on to small video interest groups, building a following along the way. Even though they missed time lines and had to raise the price on the camera well above their initial objective, they maintained a steady stream of enthusiastic customers. Today they have grown into a powerhouse in the motion picture industry, selling cameras used in a number of major motion pictures.

Summary

Product Competitive Intelligence offers a systematic approach for analyzing your products, competition, and markets, and positioning your products in a way that is most appealing to individual micro-demographics. Product Competitive Intelligence facilitates targeted marketing that permits cultivation of a broad customer base, often at much less expense than traditional marketing approaches.

Case Study: Sparkling Pools

Based on its competitive, product, and micro-demographics intelligence gathering the competitive intelligence team has determined that a number of strategies may be employed to increase its product sales, add new products, and position it as both a provider of premium pool products and also a sustainable organization.

The team follows up on their text analysis by participating in discussion groups where they have seen discussions of interest to their product development and marketing efforts. They decide to ask the members of the groups their help in development of the new products.

A significant number of pool owners and users complain about the effects of chlorine. Sparkling can develop an antimicrobial chemical treatment for pools that is chlorine free using hydrogen peroxide and other chemicals. Since there are similar chemical in the market, they will implement a two pronged approach through the premium positioning and well as sustainability. By adding a small amount of essential oils to the treatment they can also market the product as an aromatherapy solution. This will appeal to those with spas and hot tubs. They also analyzed the plastic packaging used in competing products. Due to the reactivity of the chemicals they will be forced to use plastic bottles, however there is a bottle that they can use that contains much less plastic than any of the competitors. Thus they can argue that much less plastic waste is associated with their product. In order to enhance the premium status of their new chemical line they decide to create a new brand under which it will be sold.

The existing product line can also be updated to conform to the sustainability objective by eliminating the plastic packaging in most of the products. They find that nearly all of their plastic packaging can be eliminated.

To further their sustainability goals they decide to position themselves as plastic negative by supporting efforts of groups working on removal of plastic waste from the oceans. Through their contributions, more plastic is removed than the company sells. They also offer a recycling incentive by offering customers a store credit for every plastic bottle from their product line that is returned. The side benefit of this of course is to motivate customers to come into their store and make additional purchases.

The finding that there are a large number of locals involved in water sports resulted in the company adding a line of water sports equipment such as swimming goggles, water polo equipment, and sun screen. The company decided to sponsor several teams in the area using part of its marketing budget.

The company analyzed its carbon footprint. Since the vans being used by the maintenance technicians were nearing the end of their lease terms, moving to electric vehicles would present a negative cost since the savings on fuel would more than offset the small additional lease payments arising from the move to electric vehicles. A local graphics company was hired to turn the vehicles into rolling billboards advertising the company's environmentally responsible approach.

One outcome of the research was the realization that the company sold no services online, yet there were several possible services that they might offer. One of these is consultation for problems with pools, spas, and hot tubs. The company created a test kit that customers could order, then send the results in for analysis and a recommendation on the proper treatment of their water. An added benefit of the service is increased sales of their treatment products.

Exercises

1. Visit Twitter and read the day's top tweets. Identify 10 topics of discussion. How many of these lend themselves to micro-demographic marketing? How might you reach those markets?

2. List 3 trends that you have observed over the past year. How could you market into those trends?

3. List 3 hot button issues that have an associated discussion groups and Twitter followings. How could you market into those groups without appearing to spam the group?

5

Defining Products and Services

Defining Product and Services

Often one of the most difficult parts of analysis in Product Competitive Intelligence is determining exactly what the product is that is being analyzed. If you are making and selling widgets then that is pretty simple, however as you start combining products or adding services into the mix things start getting fuzzy. We will also delve into a further complexity with the idea of systems in the next chapter. For now, let's decide if you are selling a product or a service, and then break that down into other constituent parts for analysis. First, if your customer is hiring you to do something, then you are most likely providing a service. If they are hiring you to deliver a finished product of some sort then that's probably a product. Let's take a look at wedding photography. You are being hired to photograph the wedding. You are also delivering a finished product. You may also sell prints to others in the family such as parents. This is a tough call. Some wedding photographers break it down so there is a charge for the service of photographing the wedding separate from products in the form of albums and photos that are sold separately. This is probably the best approach in terms of analysis as we can then look at a set of attributes associated with albums, photographs, and photographer services separately. Often there are internal and external distinctions, such as when a company has products and services in separate divisions. The customer may think of the company as providing a service even though the product component of the invoice might be much higher than the service component.

Divide and Conquer

A key to analyzing products or services is breaking everything down into the basic products and/or services that are being sold. A wedding album has some number of photographs included, however the unit being sold is the album. Separate photos that are sold fall into another product category. Different weddings might have need for different levels of service, for instance the wedding ceremony might be followed by a big reception needing several hours of coverage. Attributes for the album are things like dimensions, materials used in construction, and the number and sizes of photos. Attributes of photos include dimensions, print finishing, and type of print. Attributes of the wedding photography service might include number of hours, number of photographers, and type of cameras used. A photographer analyzing the competitive situation could compare offerings based on these dimensions. In the marketing material for these competitors additional dimensions might be discovered. Likewise, additional dimensions might be revealed through the interview process with prospective clients who might ask about details of the services and products provided for which prior analysis had not been considered. An additional place to look for dimensions and triggers of interest to customers is on social media channels that target a particular interest. In the case of wedding photographers, looking at Facebook groups and similar forums frequented by brides would be informative in this respect.

Systems are combinations of products and/or services which are combined and sold as some type of unit. As previously mentioned, wedding photography is a candidate for analysis as a system. However, prior to analyzing the system, it is important to analyze the components of the system. So, whether in the end analysis you are selling a product, service, or a system comprising multiple products and/or services, break things down into individual products and services for the purpose of analysis.

Features and attributes will appeal to various market segments in different ways.

Products

The key differentiator between a product and service is physicality. Most products are things of some sort. They can be virtual things like data, as in a digital image, but in most cases a product is a physical object, whether it is an apple or an automobile. Products have physical attributes such as quantity, size, and color. There are other distinguishing characteristics that we will delve into later when we explore features and attributes in detail. From these physical attributes and metrics such as price we can also determine derivative statistics such as cost per use.

Services

The difference between a product and a service is somewhat like that between a noun and a verb. Services usually imply some type of action or activity. It might involve labor or work that is performed by a person. It might be an automated process or the enabling of a product. A cell phone is of little use until it is subscribed to a cellular service. In many cases a service is something simple like window cleaning or shoe shining. Services also have attributes similar to products. Those attributes may be quantifiers associated with the service, such as the number of windows that will be cleaned, or the amount of grass that will be cut, or the maximum number of gigabytes of data that may be served.

Product Utilizing Services

Since cell phones were mentioned in relation to services we might create a special category or two where a product is tightly integrated with a service. As we'll see later this can also be treated as a system. At the product and service level we can see how the choice of a product may have a bearing on the availability of service options, and vice versa. A cell phone utilizes a cellular service. Cell phones have capabilities in addition to making phone calls. Most are able to send text messages. Some are "smart phones" which have additional features such as ability to access the Internet. That capability is contingent on the availability of the carrier to provide this service and the consumer's willingness to pay for it.

Services Utilizing Products

While the distinction might be somewhat fuzzy or open to debate, we can assert that there are services that utilize products. For instance, a pool maintenance service might utilize a set of products such as antibacterial chemicals and algae treatments. Again, the service and product options and attributes may be mutually dependent.

Case Study: Sparkling Pools

As part of its intelligence gathering efforts the competitive intelligence team decided to perform a deep analysis on the products they sell and services they offer. As part of their maintenance services they provide their branded products, making this a service utilizing products. However, with the addition of the new premium line of products, they consider either separating the products and services and making them separately billed line items, adding premium services that include the upgraded products, or making the premium products upgrade options on the existing services. They decide to test market the three different approaches to different customers to see which approach yields the highest conversion to the new product line.

Exercise

1. Pick 3 products and describe them in terms of their attributes.

2. Pick 3 services and describe them in terms of their attributes.

3. What products do you use that require a service?

4. What services do you use that use or require one or more products?

6

Data Acquisition

Product Competitive Intelligence is a data intensive process. Data is accumulated from competitive intelligence, product intelligence, micro-demographic research, and other Product Competitive Intelligence related activities. There are many sources of this data. Let's examine a few of these. This is not intended to be a comprehensive list but provides a place to start with research.

Product Labels

Product labels are a treasure trove of data. They contain information such as the UOM, the UPC code, ingredients, warnings, instructions for use, and place of manufacture.

In some cases you may be able to find product label data online, either as a product photograph or on the manufacturer's website.

Company Website

Company websites contain information on products they manufacture, often data that is not found on the label. One important document is safety data containing a description of hazards associated with chemicals in products. This safety data may be particularly pertinent in targeting micro-demographics for whom particular product ingredients may be a concern due to allergy, cancer risk, or potential environmental impact.

MSDS and Other Safety Data

Safety data can provide insight into formulations of products in addition to the safety issues associated with those ingredients. Customers are often unaware of the types of chemicals that are in the products that they buy. Research may be useful in discovering negative triggers that may be associated with the constituents of competitor products.

Lawsuits

Lawsuits arise from any number of reasons. The content of a legal filing can offer information regarding a competitor's business practices, safety record, and other information that may prove useful in Product Competitive Intelligence. Companies try to limit the opportunity for lawsuits by requiring arbitration in contracts, however there remain opportunities for disputes to end up in civil court.

Other Legal Filings

In order to be licensed for some activities companies may be required to file information with a government agency that may be useful. In some cases these filings may be more substantial than those filed with the SEC. A recent case in point was the data acquired by a fraud investigator looking into financial statements by General Electric. Access to some of this data may require using commercial databases that aggregate such data, however this may prove much more efficient than pursuing data via Freedom of Information Act (FOIA) filings and similar avenues.

SEC Filings

Public companies are required to file forms periodically with the SEC or similar agencies in their respective companies. Contents of these documents may reveal information regarding risk exposure, company performance, and other useful data.

Complaints

It is human nature to complain and the Internet is full of comments from those complaining on nearly any topic, your and your competitors' products included. Sometimes those complaints arise from stupidity on the part of the complainer, but sometimes they are wholly justified. If they are justified and apply to your products then you know what to do. Fix the problem. However, you can take consumer complaints about competitor products and turn that negative trigger into a positive trigger when you can show that your product does not do the thing that the competitor's product does that generates the complaint, such as "leaves a sticky mess."

Customer Comments

Customer comments have more to do with analysis of customer ratings of products than it does with complaints. What do customers like and dislike about the products?

Brochures

Product brochures and their online equivalent are another source of useful competitor data. There may be greater detail regarding the physical characteristics, usage instructions, cautionary information, and other important information that will not fit on a product label.

Historical data in brochures acquired via the Internet Archive can provide details regarding product evolution as well as information that was formerly public.

Job Boards

Career listings can provide insight into company plans, infrastructure, and strategy. In some cases a company will attempt to obfuscate their job searches using third parties to perform the search.

Patent and Trademark Filings

In seeking to protect their intellectual property companies may tip their hand as to what they are working on, as well as their long term strategy. Patent and trademark filings are useful sources of information in this respect.

Patent filings can also be used in counterintelligence. A company may attempt to mislead competitors as to their plans and strategy by filing patents for designs that they have no intention of developing. This may be used to mislead a competitor who is obsessed with a high risk venture by making it appear that their competitor has already solved the problem that they have been working on.

Social Media

Executives and employees of companies may use social media during trips that can provide clues about activities and plans associated with a company. For instance, comments left on a restaurant review site, selfies posted with others in the same company or companies that might be involved in a collaboration or merger might be useful for Product Competitive Intelligence analysis.

On technical and other professional social media sites employees of companies may post information about the projects they are working on, or have worked on. Competitive intelligence from this information or from contacts developed through research can provide additional insight.

Flight Data

FlightAware and similar databases may provide information regarding movement of executives traveling by private aircraft. Business jets must file flight plans because they travel at high altitude. Jets may be owned or leased by the company or they may be chartered, therefore it may take some sleuthing to determine likely candidates for trips between two or more points. Flights can signal negotiations between parties leading up to mergers, acquisitions, or major deals and collaborations.

Data Management

Data acquired through research may be treated similarly regardless of its source. Acquire the facts, then dimensionalize. It is advisable to keep records of where data was sourced and when it was sourced. Data provided directly by a competitor, whether on a label or the company's website should be considered authoritative when the company is making statements about its own products in the sense that it is the company making the statements.

On the other hand it is interesting when the statements are provably false, or which are contradicted by statements by the company from other official company sources. Products can have versions, so documenting which version is being referenced is important. For instance, a formulation may change based on increased (or decreased) environmental regulation.

Facts that you catalog can later be used as a source of further analysis.

Automating Data Acquisition

There are many ways of automating data acquisition for Product Competitive Intelligence. Webscraping is a process in which a computer program or script is used to traverse a website, download web pages and documents, then extract data from the files downloaded. Data can be extracted from printed materials like labels using optical character recognition (OCR) software. One caution with OCR is the fact that accuracy of the data as well as the data context are difficult to predict. In some cases a fast data entry person can outperform the best OCR software. Don't underestimate the power of a great data entry person.

Scripts are useful for data extraction and are written in computer scripting languages such as Perl and Python. *Regular expressions* are data structures used to identify information within a data file which can be used by these scripting languages to extract data, and also to transform the data extracted. Words, numbers, character patterns, and similar sequences are easily extracted with scripts and regular expressions.

Case Study: Sparkling Pools

The PCI team has accumulated a lot of competitor, product, and other data in various forms from product labels to URLs pointing to articles of interest. They need to get the data into a usable format for text mining and comparisons. They decide to hire a data entry person to import the data from product labels and other printed matter into the PCI data repository. Each label refers to a product with a UOM, product type, product name, and other attributes such as the ingredients. Most of the products also contain information such as the instructions for use. A data analyst designs a data model in which the parameters of these instructions and other information can be stored and used for future comparisons.

Exercise

1. Pick products to research and then see how much data you can accumulate on the products and their competitors.

2. Put the data in tabular form using a spreadsheet.

3. Of the data that you acquired, categorize each field as quantitative or non-quantitative.

4. For the non-quantitative data, how can you analyze to cast as quantitative? Which data can be divided into categories?

5. What process can you use to convert data that can be categorized into categories?

7

Units Of Measure

Product UOM

Every product that is sold has a unit of measure or UOM. The concept also extends to services. UOM is an important concept because it affects how products are packaged and sold, consumed, and most importantly from the perspective of Product Competitive Intelligence, compared. Packaging a product has an associated cost and that cost extends to shipping, receiving, stocking, and other overhead. Smaller quantities cost more to package and sell the same gross amount of product. Every manufacturer would love to sell face lotion by the drum at the same price they sell it in little dispensers, however consumers will not purchase larger quantities unless they receive a discount. The shelf life or usable product life of a product may vary and the variability may be influenced by exposure to air when the product is opened or similar factors. Therefore some products must be used within a short timeframe in order to be able to consume all of the product. These are important considerations in Product Competitive Intelligence, each having dimensions of comparison across competing products. Thus it is important to compare products that are close in terms of UOM. For instance, a liter is nearly the same as a quart, so close enough for comparison. However, if the quantity used in one product is much greater than the quantity used of the competing product, then a different UOM might be suggested for the comparison. A difference in usable product life might be another factor in selecting a UOM for comparison.

In most cases commodity products are compared in like UOMs, such as quarts or liters of liquid, pounds or kilos of solids. An important and often used UOM is Each, or other quantity, such as a dozen eggs.

Special UOMs

Some UOMs are highly specific to a particular type of product. Wood sold as firewood is sold by the cord or fraction thereof. A cord is 4x4x8 feet, or 128 cubic feet. Sometimes a vendor will sell it by another unit such as "pickup load", however this is a non-standard UOM. The non-standard term might have a claimed equivalence to the standard, such as "a pickup load is half a cord." Trust but verify. By one calculation the standard bed of a Ford F-150 is 55.4 cubic feet, which misses the mark by quite a bit. The public may not know the difference and is easily mislead.

Service UOMs

Service UOMs are usually based on project or time, but can have other basis. Whatever the basis, it is important to understand what is implied. "Clean your gutters" seems pretty straightforward, but many underlying questions might need to be asked in order to fully understand what that phrase implies. Does that mean all debris will be removed? What will be done with it after removal? Will the exterior of the gutters be cleaned? Will the downspouts be cleaned? How is the gutter cleaning price calculated? Does building height affect price? Ancillary questions might also be asked. Does the vendor have liability and workers compensation insurance? In order to compare service offerings it is vitally important to understand all components that make up the service being sold.

Using UOMs Competitively

Educating consumers can be to your benefit. In researching your competitors take a serious look at the assumptions that go into the descriptions of the products and services sold, and the UOMs. You can raise questions in their mind that they will want answered before choosing the competitor. They may be dynamically generating their own negative triggers in the process.

UOM Based Comparisons

When comparing products where UOM is a component in the comparison, it is useful to standardize on a Base UOM for some types of comparisons, even when referring to quantities sold in sizes other than the base UOM. For instance, if we are comparing paint that is sold in sizes ranging from a half-pint to 5 gallons, we might standardize on the gallon as the comparative unit in terms of metrics such as coverage. Thus regardless of the price, which is contingent on the size of the container, coverage is generally independent and square feet per gallon (or square meters per liter) is a common unit for measuring coverage.

System Based UOM

As analysis turns from products to systems, units of measure play a similar role and standardization is equally important. Consider a paint system consisting of a primer, base coat, and top coat. Each component in the system has metrics such as coverage and dry time. The system may have metrics such as throughput or the number of widgets that might be painted with the system per hour, the amount of paint required to paint 100 standard widgets, and the cost to paint each widget. System comparisons may be much more insightful than individual system component comparisons, even when the system comparisons are based on mathematical sums of those individual statistics. Competitors A and B compared on price alone may favor Competitor A's products, however a system comparison may find that Competitor B's system is more productive and thus the superior choice for a particular purpose.

Usage is an important criterion in comparisons at the product level. Using paint as an example again, if product A covers in one coat and product B requires two coats to achieve the same degree of coverage, this has an influence on many potential points of comparison. For instance the dry time, labor requirement, and transportation, all are increased in addition to the material cost.

Lifetime of the product is another factor to consider. For instance, a paint with a UV inhibitor might imply more years of service life before a reapplication of paint is required. Metrics such as lifetime should be based on similar standard conditions, such as a standard unit of UV exposure. Claims by manufacturers are often difficult to compare due to the choice of the basis of comparison. Comparisons in this case are useful only as far as it is possible to transform the metrics into the same units.

Base UOM

Once a Base UOM is established, a conversion factor may be defined for those products having a UOM other than the Base UOM. A conversion factor is a number that when multiplied by the unit being converted, yields the number of units in the Base UOM. For instance, if my Base UOM is Gallon and the UOM of the product is 5 Gallons, the the conversion factor is 5. If another product is sold in a UOM of Quart, then its conversion factor is .25. To compare prices and other UOM dependent quantities at the Base UOM level, then simply divide by the conversion factor.

Case Study: Sparkling Pools

The PCI team was able to import all of the competitor product data into its data repository and is ready to begin deriving comparative analysis. The competing products are sold in differing concentrations and product UOMs. The team needs every product's equivalent usage and pricing in a consistent Base UOM in order to make sensible comparisons. The products are sold as either liquids measured by volume or dry materials sold by weight and used by volume. They decide to use quart as the liquid UOM, pound as the weight UOM, and dry cup as the solid volume UOM. For each of the UOMs of products in the database they enter a conversion factor to translate the product UOM into that used for comparison.

Exercise

1. Pick a few products and examine the units of measure in which they are sold.

2. For each product pick a different UOM and express the product sizes in terms of the new UOMs.

3. What is the cost of each product in the new UOM?

4. Create a table of products, the product prices, UOM in which each product is sold, the Base UOM you will use to compare, the conversion factor for each UOM to Base UOM conversion, and the prices per Base UOM. Use a spreadsheet and formulas to minimize the amount of data entry required.

8

Unit Normalization

In the last chapter we touched on the importance of the Base UOM for product comparisons. This in essence is the basis for unit normalization. Unit normalization is the standardization of units across all comparisons. It begins with the products and services being compared and is convenient in that regard, however it becomes critical when comparisons begin to be made at the system level.

Dimensional Analysis

To understand unit normalization we need to take a side tour into dimensional analysis or DA. Everyone is familiar with units of measure and common conversion factors such as 4 quarts per gallon and 100 centimeters per meter. However, few understand that these units of measure and conversion factors can be chained together into lengthy equations to accomplish difficult conversions where no standard formula is readily available. With dimensional analysis we always start with the dimensions that we have and the dimensions that we would like to end up with at the end. For instance, let's say that a farmer sells his milk by the 13 gallon milk can at the local farmers market. Other farmers sell their milk at the market in a 10 gallon milk can. We would like to compare milk prices in 10 gallon milk can units. We will do this by multiplying the units and the conversion factors. Units and conversion factors can be in both the numerator and denominator in the equation, and they cancel out, so if you have gallon in the numerator and gallon in the denominator those will cancel out. Note that units can multiply as well as divide, which might lead to square units.

Application to Units of Measure

In our milk can example we have 13 gallon cans and we want to end up with 10 gallon cans. For brevity, lets use LC as the unit for the 13 gallon can and SC as the unit for the 10 gallon can. We have 1 LC and want to know how many that is in SC.

We know that:

1 LC = 13 Gal

1 SC = 10 Gal

Then

1 LC/ 1 SC = 13 Gal / 10 Gal = 13/10

So the Gal cancel in the second equivalence leading to a ratio of 13/10 which is our conversion factor. Now if we want to compare milk prices between the two vendors, where vendor A sells milk in the 13 gallon container for $18 and vendor B sells milk in the 10 gallon container for $15, the conversion factor for vendor A is 13/10 and the conversion factor for vendor B is 1. Dividing the respective milk prices by the conversion factors, vendor A's milk is 18/1.3 = $13.84 per SC unit and vendor B is $15.00.

As previously stated, unit normalization becomes increasingly important with system comparisons. Systems can be exceedingly complex, so every means of simplifying things can help illustrate the differences between systems clearly. A comparison of paint systems might include a comparison of throughput, a measurement that would have as its basis some standardization in terms of the size of the widgets.

Case Study: Sparkling Pools

In order to compare products between competitors the PCI team determined the factorization methods for each unit encountered in the products. Product UOMs included liter, quart, pint, liquid ounce, kilogram, and pound.

Exercise

1. Tom can paint 4 hectares per fortnight. How many square feet can he paint per hour?

2. 36 grains of propellant accelerates a 1 lb. projectile to 1800 feet per second. Express this in metric terms using grams for mass and meters for distance. What is the projectile velocity in miles per hour?

3. Compare two paint systems. Each system is comprised of a primer coat, color coat, and top coat. Assume that each widget being painted is 3.7 square feet. Which system is more productive in terms of the number of widgets that can be painted per hour? Which system has the lowest cost per widget? In terms of production, all other factors being equal (i.e. both paint systems produce the same quality), when would it be more advantageous to use one system over another? Assume that you can sell every widget that you can produce.

Ven-dor	Coating	Coverage	Dry Time	Price
A	Primer	38 ft²/qt	1.5 hour	$32/qt
A	Color	160 ft²/qt	4 hour	$64/qt
A	Top	240 ft²/qt	3.0 hour	48/qt
B	Primer	37 m²/l	2.0 hour	$36/l
B	Color	64 m²/l	4.5 hour	$57/l
B	Top	120 m²/l	2.0 hour	$87/l

9

Features and Attributes

Features and attributes are at the root of comparisons. Whether you sell a product or service there are facts about the product or service that can be used to compare competing products and services. Let's examine the nature of products and services and see how the features and attributes can be cataloged and used in comparisons.

Attributes

Products have physical attributes. Each attribute set is particular to the type of product. Shirts have different attributes than jars of jelly. That's not to say that different types of products can't share attributes, such as size or unit of measure. However shirts don't have a flavor, usually. And jelly doesn't have a sleeve length. Products have features that distinguish them from other products. If they didn't they would be commodities, although commodities may have distinguishing characteristics. Is a pound of sand only a pound of sand, or is it a pound of white sand containing 80% quartzite? The key in finding and enumerating attributes is finding those that the products should share, then determining their values. In some cases a value is not stated by the manufacturer and only becomes of interest in the context of a comparison. In other cases a claim is made by the manufacturer but needs to be verified by a third party. For instance, a maker of ink for inkjet printers and photographic paper may make a claim that their paper and ink combination has a color life expectancy of 200+ years. They may or may not publish their testing methodology. A third party that independently tests paper and ink combinations and that is not paid by the manufacturer, may test the paper and ink combination and corroborate or dispute the manufacturer's claim.

Features

Another aspect of product comparisons is features. Whereas attributes tend to be physical properties, features can be more abstract descriptions like "fast drying" or "easy to use". Features are often referred to as benefits, but in some cases they might be disadvantages or limitations. The desirability of a feature may vary between consumers. Desirability or perceived benefit of the feature may be associated with a value proposition. For instance, plastic-free packaging has a variable desirability depending on one's degree of concern regarding plastic pollution. Although there may be some fuzziness to features, in order to be compared those features must be comparable in some manner. If two products claim ease of use, which is the easier to use? If both are fast drying, which dries faster? These may require independent testing.

Independent Testing

Independent testing in comparative analysis must be done properly if the results are to be believed. There are many reviews posted on YouTube in which the reviewers may condemn a product they are testing or promote its benefits. They may feature a "shootout" of various competing products. However, rigorous independent testing should go beyond this, letting an independent third party develop and publish a testing methodology which any other tester could recreate and verify the results. For instance, let's say we wanted to establish that our product is faster drying than all competing products. We employ a test lab. The test lab might source the samples rather than have us provide them, so as to avoid any bias with respect to sample selection. Then the lab would develop a test procedure for applying the products, drying the products, and measuring dryness. The lab would then test each product using the methodology and report the results.

Exclusivity

Some features of a product may be exclusive to that product. Exclusivity can exist due to innovation, protection by patent, or disinterest by competition. Exclusivity can be fuzzy, meaning that a competing product's feature may be similar to the feature that is exclusive. For instance, two pigments may claim to be the blackest black. Yet each is exclusive through a patent on the particular formulation. An independent test might reveal that either is the blackest within the error ranges of the measuring equipment and thus may not be able to prove conclusively that one is blacker than the other.

Service Attributes

Like products, services have characteristics that may be measured or described, which we can refer to as service attributes. Like products, these attributes are specific to the type of service being performed. For instance a gutter cleaning service will have specific attributes, such as number of downspouts, size of house, and disposal of waste as the attributes associated with a gutter cleaning price.

Services may have features or benefits, such as "fast service" or "on time delivery" which, like product features, might have to be independently tested.

Sources of Feature and Attribute Data

Where will we find features, attributes, and benefits? There are several sources we will turn to when we begin to tabulate them for comparison.

- Labels
- Advertising
- Brochures
- Manufacturer website
- User reviews and comments
- Patent filings
- Public filings
- Instructions, user guides, and manuals

Quantitative Comparisons

When looking for limitations and disadvantages of competing products, you may need to analyze documents such as the user guides and instructions for comparison. For instance, application of one paint primer may require more extensive prep work than the competing brand. This could be cast in different ways. Ease of use might be the benefit of the product for which the prep work is not required.

In many cases we have what we might call soft descriptions of features that make them difficult to compare across competitors. Turn these soft descriptions into numeric or categorical quantities for comparison, using a mode that is appropriate. A boolean might be used to say whether or not a feature exists. A sliding scale can be used to quantify imprecise statements like ease of use. For instance in comparing ease of use, 10 participants in the study would rank each product on a 1 to 5 scale, and the ratings averaged. Similarly reviews may be ranked in a like manner.

How do we structure comparisons? A common approach in structuring comparisons is a tabular attribute-by-attribute comparison. We see these on shopping sites where you can select products to compare and their attributes are listed in columns. Some comparisons need to be more complex, particularly when our focus is on the feature set and certain feature comparisons require detailed analysis, or when they have contextual considerations. A product may be superior for a particular use under certain conditions. Two cameras may be claimed to be water resistant by the manufacturers. How water resistant are they? Let's take them to the jungle during monsoon and find out. Such field tests are not controlled lab tests and shouldn't be confused as such, but they can be real world accounts of experiences of a user that reflect the reality that a photojournalist might face if she were sent to Borneo to photograph betel chewing culture.

Superiority Metrics

Another approach to structuring comparisons is to build a case for a product using selected comparative statistics to support the superiority of one product over another. This we refer to as superiority metrics. Attributes and features are analyzed with the intent to position a product as the superior choice as proven by the chosen metrics. Those superiority metrics may be specific to particular value propositions and the arguments are constructed in support of those propositions. For instance, a value proposition might be Zero Plastic Waste. In comparison, the plastic waste produced in the use of each product may be calculated using statistics on expected utilization over a year.

Other comparisons may be derived from multiple product attributes, features, and instructions for use. For instance, suppose you are comparing your product to another and want to show that your product is less expensive to use than the competitor's similar product, even though your product is priced higher. This may be because your product is used at a different dilution, or because it requires fewer applications. Simple tabular comparisons such as price per UOM fail to make such important distinctions. Choose your tabular comparisons carefully.

It may help to provide proof that your generic feature is true in comparison to your competitor. If the feature is "Better for the environment", there may be multiple specific things that make your product better for the environment, so spell those out. In addition to Zero Plastic Waste, your product might also produce Lowest VOC Emissions.

Look beyond attributes and features to the raw materials used in products in order to find additional distinguishing characteristics. Do your competitors' products contain dangerous chemicals? Might the raw materials or the products themselves have been sourced from slave labor? If the competing product really manufactured in the USA or was it merely assembled there using foreign manufactured parts? If the product is of foreign manufacture and is a critical component in a primary customer's manufacturing process, is it at risk to a supply disruption to which you are not subject?

Case Study: Sparkling Pools

The PCI team decides to take another pass through the competing products using the intelligence that they have gathered. They derive total cost per year of each competing product based on a standard pool size and the instructions from the manufacturer. They weigh the plastic packaging from each competitor's product and calculate the plastic waste produced using the product over a year.

The team is interested in consumer perceptions associated with the products. They hire a survey firm to conduct a blind independent survey of all competing products. The survey is conducted to measure the participants' opinion of product labeling, importance of environmental factors such as plastic waste, product odors, desirability of aromatherapy options, pricing, and interest in the premium product line.

Exercise

1. Describe a product or service that you sell or plan to sell. What are its attributes and features?

2. Describe a competitor's product or service that would compete with the product or service you described in 1. What are its attributes and features?

3. Compare both products or services at a tabular level. Construct arguments using the facts you have at hand that position your product or service as superior to that of your competitor. Are you missing any information that would assist you in further establishing your product's or service/s superiority over your competitor? How might you acquire that information?

10

Superiority Metrics

Features and attributes of products, services, and systems represent a vast landscape across which comparisons may be drawn. Comparisons may be quantitative or qualitative and represent distinctions and categories of interest, either alone or in combination. The end goal of these comparisons is the derivation of criteria which may be used to establish the superiority of one product, service, or system over another with respect to criteria that are important to, or holds validity within, specific market segments.

Special Interest Segmentation

Social media and other Internet based communications such as forums and news groups have contributed greatly to the development of highly segmented special interest areas where people tend to congregate. As an example, those interested in environmental issues tend to self-aggregate by following certain people on Twitter, membership in environmental groups such as the Sierra Club and Greenpeace, and participation in environmental forums on Facebook. The desirability of products or certain features of products is often directly related to the predominant memes within these groups. Consequently, the superiority metrics derived from product comparisons will be based on these special criteria. Using this approach, product differentiation can occur based on the dimensions of importance to the areas of greatest interest.

Let's illustrate this with an example of how we might establish superiority metrics for a product that we produce. The product is a common object that people might consider a staple or commodity, therefore there is little price differentiation. We are looking for an angle that will appeal to a broad group of consumers. We note that 90% of the competing products are packaged in plastic and in every case the plastic does not have a recycling symbol. The product is something that is used daily by all members of a household. Therefore we can estimate the consumption for a family of four over one year. Our differentiating criteria will be plastic packaging, and more generally the concept of sustainability. We know that, for our target market, the interest in sustainability is high and follows a standard distribution in some respects, so we expect a very strong interest in some parts of the demographic. Therefore, the label on the product should point out the environmentally responsible justification for choosing the product. We can use social media influencers within the target demographics to build interest in the product based on the superiority metrics that we have defined. For instance, someone who is an activist in the area of plastic pollution might commend your use of non-plastic packaging. You can build a stronger meme around this by seeking advice from this and other consumers within that demographic. Although you might have pre-determined the outcome of such an interaction, you actually may gain additional insight regarding the packaging that you intend to use in place of plastic. For instance, what if the use of certain types of inks, and the paper used in label and packaging produced additional incentives for this consumer base to purchase your products? You might not be aware of certain triggers contained within your carefully designed environmentally responsible business strategy.

Expressing For Impact

Superiority metrics can be expressed in a more impactful way depending on how they are formulated. Tons of plastic waste sent to landfills annually using a competing product is much stronger than saying your product produces no plastic waste. Look at the impact a large number of users, say 1 million, might have on the environment. Even when the competitor is using a recyclable plastic, there are still strong statistics to be drawn pertaining to the actual amount of recyclable plastic that never makes it to a recycling plant. Once you have established a strong case and have buy-in and recommendations from thought leaders in the target demographic it is a simple jump to expand the reach of this message to a larger audience and the marketing message is deployed where it will be most effective. The value proposition doesn't have to wait to be discovered. It can be deployed in new products and revisions to existing ones.

Using Value Propositions

Demographics often involves categorization according to age, sex, income, education, zip code, ethnicity, etc. The expanded demographics that take special interests into account and profiles that define target groups do not have to have identifying data. In other words we can market blindly to these stratifications in some contexts without knowing anything else about the group members. Knowing the likely positive and negative triggers may be sufficient.

A value proposition that is specific to the values held dear by those in the target demographic may have a defined set of important selection criteria relevant to them. The value proposition and marketing is designed to address that specific set of values.

Analytical Tools

We can employ data science to find metrics of interest. Data science has become as much a buzz phrase as AI and machine learning has, but essentially we want to use data to provide insights. Finding data is easy. The challenge is using it in a way that produces the insights we seek. Companies acquire a lot of data and there is much data in the public domain and available for purchase. You may already have a lot of customer data. Data science is just a formal methodology for putting that data to work. It can also be used to provide insight into competitive product statistics, for instance clusters and outliers in dry times for paint might yield useful comparisons. Data science provides great tools for Product Competitive Intelligence. The visual display of quantitative information conveys understanding more quickly than detailed descriptions. For instance a plot of numeric values such a paint dry times might be a more effective visual than a tabular comparison since people prefer to look at pictures and love looking at graphs. Use infographics for full effect. Use data science to analyze target demographics as well.

Does AI have a place in comparative metrics? AI seems to be everywhere you look these days and it is being put to wide use. AI allows you to find hidden relationships in data. Like any tool it is possible to become a crutch for those too lazy to perform more fundamental research or who fail to understand the underlying relationships driving the outputs from the algorithms being employed. It may be difficult to determine the important factors at play in establishing product superiority and is therefore worth investigation, perhaps after the normal analysis has concluded. Intuitive and easy to understand concepts will be more convincing to a customer in addressing their specific high value concerns.

Case Study: Sparkling Pools

The Sparkling Pools PCI team learns a great deal from comparing features of their products with those of their competitors. The reduction of plastic in packaging will result in a strong superiority metric over the competition and the survey results reflected the strength of this positive trigger across a broad range of consumers, not just those who identified as environmental activists.

In many cases the annual cost of some of Sparkling Pools treatment chemicals were lower than competing brands, and in others they were slightly higher. The team starting working on ideas for value propositions that would position the higher priced products better in consumers' minds. The premium product line with its aromatherapy option helped, but the team wanted a more generally appealing superiority metric. The team decided to pay for an independent lab to perform tests on the competing chemicals. They wanted to know which products were best in terms of antimicrobial function and determine if there were other metrics the lab might apply. The results from the lab made the effort worth the expense. There were two important findings. First, the Sparkling Pools products produced the lowest microbial count of all competing products used according to the manufacturers' directions. Second, water clarity was higher with the Sparkling Pools chemicals. The pools were really sparkling. This provided excellent material for building the value propositions.

Exercise

1. Name 3 micro-demographics. For each one list 2 or 3 values that are characteristic of that population.

2. For each value listed in 1, without naming a specific product, name as many product metrics that you can employ as positive or negative triggers to cause a member of the population to purchase the product.

3. Using the comparative metrics derived in 2, can you think of two competing products for which you can construct an argument in support of one over the other for each of the micro-demographics?

11

Defining the Value Proposition

A key concept in Product Competitive Intelligence is establishing the positive and negative triggers that are characteristic of the micro-demographics comprising the target market and then delivering one or more value propositions that assert those triggers while a purchase decision is being considered. In order to do so we need to determine who would be interested in purchasing the product or service and then determine how that customer base is segmented socially, politically, and by special interests.

Market Analysis

A good first step is determination of the customer base who are likely to purchase and use your product or service. For instance, if you are offering a pool cleaning service for swimming pools, then the customer base might include homeowners with pools.

Additional market research might result in additional types of customers, such as homeowners with spas and hot tubs. It might also reveal that hotels, clubs, and exercise facilities are prospects for pool maintenance services, perhaps by demonstrating to them the benefits of outsourcing the service.

List the potential special interests of those who may be using the product, whether the special interest is associated with its use or selection of the product might hinge on criteria that are specific to those in that interest group. For instance, might plastic packaging, BPA content, release of volatile organic compounds, cost, and ROI be factors? Use these criteria as your positive and negative triggers. For instance, in the pool service example a criterion might be the use of chlorine for an antibacterial agent. Perhaps you have a chemistry that replaces chlorine with ozone treatments. Some customers may have an issue with allergies and look for pool chemistries that are hypo-allergenic.

For the triggers that you have defined within your target customers, perform a product competitive analysis on your product and on your competitors' products. Extract every single fact you can find that is remotely related to these triggers. Sometimes an obscure bit of information may become relevant to your process.

Dimensional Analysis

Using the data extracted from your product data sources, find the dimensions of interest within the different customer concerns that have been listed.

Document the features, benefits, competitor issues, and other criteria that supports the value of your brand in the context of each trigger that has been defined.

It is not necessary to name competitors in these value propositions, particularly when your product or service is an outlier compared to the competition. Back to our pool cleaning example, we might be able to state "Bob's Pool Service is the only service in the Metro area featuring chlorine-free water treatment using the patented BioGard UV water sterilization system."

In our discussion of micro-demographics we refer to special interest groups. Sometimes these are associated with social or political activism and environmental issues. But sometimes, or often, they are associated with the use of the product itself. If you are looking for the pain points of pool owners, find pool owner groups online and read their comments. Perform a text analysis on the past year's articles that members have written. In a similar fashion, a wedding photographer should analyze what prospective and new brides write about wedding photography.

Characteristics of Special Interest Groups

News groups and forums have a particular dynamic that appears consistent across interests. There are a few vocal folks who may or may not know much, but they comment on nearly everything. There are a few bullies who attack others, taking words and phrases out of context, and trying to stir the pot. There are a few intelligent folk who provide useful answers, and there is the occasional visitor who drops by in search of a solution to a problem. In nearly every special interest group there will be competing memes of some sort, and with them some associated vendor or technology. Someone always has a favorite, particularly where technology or a brand is involved. The technology may be expensive, and effort may be involved in convincing others that the thing being promoted is the only thing worth having. It's hard to know whether the meme is the work of the manufacturer, but it is always a possibility. If your objective is to usurp the holder of the favorite meme title, then you have your work cut out for you in overcoming the arguments that will be made in favor of the competitor. You know what those arguments will be because you have done your research. Often the proponent of the dominant meme will have an antagonist. This may be the person to lead your charge.

Defining your value proposition means that you have determined the values of the participants in your marketplace, have found the appropriate triggers associated with those values and have crafted your message that asserts the superiority of your product or service in terms of those values. At the heart of a value proposition is the superiority metric. A superiority metric is a property, measurement, or characteristic of your product that is measurably superior to your competitor. It can be a NOT relationship, for example you might state that the product is NOT packaged in plastic, unlike the competing product.

Case Study: Sparkling Pools

The PCI team had determined that there were a few categories of customers:

• Owners of pools, spas, and hot tubs
• Persons with allergies or sensitivity to chlorine
• Those sufficiently concerned about the environment that plastic packaging, carbon neutrality, and vendor sustainability were a consideration in a purchase.
• Those who used alternative remedies such as aroma-therapy

Using the superiority metrics they had derived, they designed the value propositions that would appeal to each of these sets of customers. The value proposition for the owners would be the increased purity and clarity of the water treated with the Sparkling Pools chemicals as proven by an independent third party laboratory. The value proposition for those with allergies and chlorine sensitivity would be the hypo allergenic properties of the premium branded pool chemistry. The value proposition for those who were environmentally aware would be the company's commitment to sustainability, reduction of its own plastic waste contribution and contribution to plastic waste reduction projects. The value proposition to those who used alternative remedies would be the availability of the aromatherapy products.

Exercise

1. Visit a news group or Internet forum on any topic and read the messages posted over the past month. Choose a forum that has a lot of traffic, say at least 100 posts per day.

2. Make a list of the different categories of people posting. Who comments a lot? Who is abusive or abrasive? Who provides sensible advice and comments?

3. What are the hot topics on the forum?

4. Are there any brands or technologies that appear to be mentioned frequently? List those and their relative occurrence (infrequent or frequent).

5. How might you position a product so that it would appeal to the members of the news group?

12

Product Comparison

Finding Comparative Dimensions

It is human nature to compare things. People compare features, their own with those of others, and features of products and services that they buy. It may surprise many that price is not the overriding criteria for purchase for many people. It is often a factor in a purchase, but other criteria may hold more weight. Comparisons are often multidimensional, meaning there can be many factors to consider, some of which may be at odds such as quality and price. We don't list features and find distinguishing characteristics of products for the fun of it, we try to find the best product at the best price, or at least at an afford-able price. Therefore when deriving comparative data we should attempt to find those distinctions which a customer is most likely to use as criteria for choosing your product over that of competitors. That is the basis for finding the positive and negative triggers associated with value propo-sitions for the consumers in the micro-demographics we hope to turn into customers.

We should make a distinction between price versus cost. Price we generally associate with the purchase of the product and cost we associate with the use of the product. In many cases they are one in the same, however in some situations there may be quite a difference. The simplest example would be in the use of competing products need-ing differing degrees of dilution. A recent trend has been the sale of concentrated solutions such as window cleaner advertised to reduce the amount of plastic waste. If the concentrate makes 5 gallons of cleaner then it would be a faulty approach to compare the price per ounce of the con-centrate with the competitor's product sold premixed. In this case like many others the comparison is an aggregate function based on more than price per unit of measure.

Aggregate Functions

Suitability for purpose is another type of comparison that may require an aggregate function to clearly articulate. Let's continue with liquid cleaners as an example. Cleaners may be a complex formulation of surfacants, solvents, and a carrier such as water which may be used at full concentration or mixed prior to application. The cleaner may be formulated to target certain types of materials such as grease and oil, or tree sap. It may also be designed to be used on certain types of surfaces, or the directions may indicate that it is explicitly not designed for certain surfaces. A glass cleaner with ammonia would not be intended for use on Plexiglas, in which it might induce crazing. In a comparison matrix one might list a product in each column, a surface on each row, and then use a check mark to indicate that the formula is suitable for the surface, and likewise for the categories of materials the formulations can clean. Thus we can establish suitability for purpose of competing products.

Abstract Comparisons

When your product is clearly more expensive than the competition, it is worthwhile to provide a rationale, or at least an excuse, for spending the extra dough. Is a Cartier watch better than a Timex? Why? Throw your price shoppers a bone and provide them with some justification for the extra expense. Most of the examples of features we examined earlier such as ease of use had some type of underlying physical property or usability consideration that established the distinction. How do you make the argument for style and sophistication? Some marketing ventures into abstract concepts by necessity. There might be an appeal to one's image or self worth. At the basis of these comparisons is some type of value proposition. The distinction is only visible when it is illuminated by the value placed on it by the consumer. Value extends beyond price into these abstract concepts such as style and sophistication. There are those who don't value style or sophistication and for them it can be concluded they are not the market for Cartier watches. On the other hand these same consumers may value punctuality, and for them a Timex might just be the perfect choice.

The question then in establishing the comparisons, as the value propositions are being considered, is what do the people in this micro-demographic value and how do we take advantage of this in our comparisons?

Niche Markets

In establishing a position of superiority within a micro-demographic it may be apparent that one is marketing into a niche, and in fact the product may be the only or best choice for everyone in that niche. Niche markets are great and many successful people are successful because they dominate a specific niche. A flight instructor specializes in training pilots to land the Pitts Special biplane. If you want to learn to land the Pitts, he is the go to guy for that task. It is a very tricky plane to land, so having an expert that can share information on its quirks will help you become a better Pitts pilot, and faster.

Try to avoid negativity when creating comparisons and structure comparisons in a favorable light. Any comparison might be cast as positive or negative, so try to express it positively even when delivering bad news about your competitor. Can you show an advantage you have that illustrates your point?

The Greatest Thing Ever!

Hyperbole can be a fun way to express a comparison. Looking at annual use by a large population permits extrapolation to make your point more impactful.

"If the plastic containers sold by the other manufacturers were placed end to end they would stretch around the Earth 3 times."

"Our encryption is so good it would take a hacker 3 trillion years to crack it."

Using Recognized Authorities

In some cases it is a third party who should be delivering comparisons in order for the comparison to carry more weight. This is especially true if the information can be categorized as a negative review of a competitor's product. There are many potential third party means of delivering comparisons, such as YouTube, social media, news groups, blogs such as Medium, reviews, articles, and lab reports. A third party engaged to distribute comparative information about your products or services should include the factual evidence on which statements are based. The more authority with which the source speaks, and the greater their reputation the more benefit you are likely to gain. They should include disclaimers as to their affiliation or lack of affiliation with your company. As always, deploy news where it will be relevant. There is no need, and it is hardly practical, to publish every fact in every venue. In fact it would be smarter to drop small tidbits here and there. Various facts coming from a variety of sources would lead a potential customer to being negatively influenced toward the competitor.

Case Study: Sparkling Pools

In determining the comparative dimensions of the different products they sell, the PCI team started with classifications of competing treatments based on suitability to purpose. Some products fell into multiple categories while some were very specialized or used to solve a particular problem. The chemical might be used on a continuous basis to keep the pool chemistry in line, or it might be used once during a season. The team also looked at more abstract comparisons such as ease of use. Sparkling Pools brands had the upper hand on some of these comparisons by supplying a ready to use dose in a sealed packet. All the owner had to do was open the package and pour the product into the water, versus the competition's approach of providing the chemical in a plastic bottle with a separate measuring device that had to be cleaned after each use. The waste produced using the competitors' products was also higher. The earlier independent lab tests provided results showing the effectiveness of the Sparkling Pools products was higher and resulted in water with more clarity.

Exercise

1. Pick a product for analysis. Who are the competitors? What are the competing products?

2. Create a comparison of the products using dimensions of your choice.

3. Create a comparison that uses an aggregate function.

4. Create a true buy hyperbolic claim regarding one of the products.

5. Pick 2 or 3 micro-demographics in which you might market one of the products. Who are their thought leaders? How might you obtain a third party analysis of the product by one of these thought leaders?

13

The Role of Systems

Systems come into play whenever products or services are combined and sold as a solution to a problem. If you have a yard service that offers a combination of lawn mowing, weed control, and plant trimming then you are most likely selling a system.

System: any combination of products and services used to achieve an objective

In some cases it is the customer that creates the system from products and services from multiple sources. Using the yard service example, they may use one vendor for weed control and another for the remaining services in order to arrive at a yard maintenance system.

Competitive intelligence may uncover opportunities to expand a simple product or service into a system solution. Customers would rather deal with one vendor if possible, especially when having to coordinate the acquisition and scheduling of services or sourcing products from multiple vendors. It sometimes requires altering one's perspective to a system view when one has been too narrowly focused.

As with the interpretation of competing product attributes and features in relation to the value propositions of interest to micro-demographics, similar attribute and feature analysis at the system level can lead to improved marketability of the system, and also reveal new markets for that system. For instance, by changing the perspective of the lawn maintenance company to a more systemic view of lawn maintenance one may arrive at a number of constituent services that comprise a comprehensive lawn maintenance system. In reviewing the features and attributes of the system in reference to the positive and negative triggers associated with the micro-demographics of interest, it might be noted that appeal to those with strong environmental concerns might be greatly increased by implementing a totally green solution. This green solution might feature the use of battery powered tools, solar charging facilities used to recharge the batteries back at the home office, and the use of natural pesticides and weed control chemicals that are pet safe. (Notice how we snuck that additional micro-demographic of pet owners into the mix?) The battery powered tools are also going to produce less noise pollution in addition to having a smaller carbon footprint. The annoyance of gasoline powered weed trimmers and leaf blowers is quite universal.

System analysis may be used to demonstrate your superiority over your competitors even when it appears to be counter intuitive, such as a system that costs more but saves the customer money. Dimensional comparisons may be discrete, multivariate, or summary in nature.

A systems analysis will expose comparative dimensions that are not obvious at the product and service level. Look at the characteristics associated with the system that point to benefits, e.g. annual cost comparison based on frequency of use, productivity, and similar benefits that arise through the use of the system. Benefits that arise only through the use of the system provide the strongest marketing messages.

Many organizations produce great products that are not part of any system and may have no desire to expand into systems. That does not imply there are no systems opportunities for these organizations. Strategic partnerships with organizations that do have a system view are one approach. Analysis that includes looking at product use as part of a system may yield discovery of potential partners. The producer of the natural weed killer might partner with the green lawn maintenance company. Systems based vendors thus comprise a marketable micro-demographic for product and service companies.

As Schaeffer and Sovie point out in *Reinventing the Product: How to Transform your Business and Create*

Value in the Digital Age, hardware-centric companies need to extend their thinking to a platform strategy that facilitates implementation of digital technology.[1] While it may not be practical to employ IoT or similar integration in some products, there is ample opportunity for doing so with many products. Consider the usefulness of your product to your consumer or to others as either a data source or sink. How might your product work with others to achieve something new and valuable? The early IoT use case was the refrigerator that would add milk to the grocery list when it detected the milk level was getting low. Modern platforms have become more sophisticated. For instance your fitness tracker might integrate with a health platform that suggests diet and exercise modifications. The health platform might also integrate with special tools such as glucose monitors for those needed to track glucose levels and suggest diet and exercise based on that data.

Case Study: Sparkling Pools

The PCI team took a system view of its products and services in order to derive additional comparative metrics with those of competitors. The found that they fundamentally had two systems. The first was the combination of chemicals that comprised the full treatment capabilities offered by Sparkling Pools. The second was the maintenance service that used the chemicals sold by the company.

Exercise

1. Pick a product at random and list its features and attributes.

2. How can the product be used in a system?

3. Construct a system using the product along with any other products and services that would be appropriate.

4. What are the attributes and features of the system?

---

1 Eric Schaeffer, David Sovie - *Reinventing the Product: How to Transform your Business and Create Value in the Digital Age,* 2019

14

System Dimensions

In PCI we distinguish between product and service metrics which yield 1:1 comparisons at the most granular level, and system metrics which yield comparisons of products and services combined in performance of their intended use. This is done because, although a product by product comparison of two competitors' products may provide one conclusion, the system comparison may produce the opposite. For instance, in the paint system comparison previously referenced, one might conclude based on the product comparison that one product line is more expensive than the competitor's products. However, upon analysis of the system that employs these products, one might find that ones productivity is greatly increased using the more expensive product line and that a business using that product line will be more profitable doing so. This is not simply a matter of selectively choosing which metrics to share, but to build a case for superiority in as many dimensions as possible.

System Versus Product Dimensions

It is interesting that system dimensions, although derived in many cases from product level dimensions, may be quite different in specifying properties of the system. The example we have been using is cost versus profitability. However there might be any number of derivative statistics. Look for dimensions of interest within the set of potential positive and negative triggers characteristic of a micro-demographic for which the analysis is being derived.

A system objective has measurable features, quantities, advantages and outcomes. A widget painting system might have dimensions such as number of widgets painted per day, cost to paint each widget, amount of waste water produced for each widget painted, etc. Dimensions are often derived from the sums of product dimensions within the context of the stated use case, for instance painting a widget, or cleaning a swimming pool.

System Dimensions and Triggers

Aside from suitability for purpose, system dimensions may be associated with positive or negative triggers within the context of a target micro-demographic. Since we have been using pollution as a key negative trigger in our examples, let's stick with that example. In comparing systems we might look at the total waste produced when painting 1,000 widgets. We might break that down into types of pollution, such as recyclable and non-recyclable plastic, volatile organic compounds released, non-plastic waste, and waste water.

Case Study: Sparkling Pools

After performing a basic system analysis the PCI team begins analyzing the dimensions of the systems that it sells. An important dimension to every consumer is time. The team compared the time required using each competitors products as a system and found that, in part due to the packaging it started using to reduce its plastic waste footprint, consumers would spend less time each day using the Sparkling Pools system. The team totaled the time savings and found a compelling statistic that more than a day could be saved.

Another important dimension for consumers is price. Earlier product analysis found that while some of the products Sparkling Pools sold had a lower cost per use, others did not. The team looked at the annual cost of using their system compared to the competition and found that consumers would save money using their entire suite of products for maintaining their pools, spas, and hot tubs.

Exercise

1. Consider cell phone service as a system and gather comparative data across the cellular providers in your area.

Include the phones available in the plans offered in your analysis.

2. Which system units of measure exist in your cellular carrier comparison?

3. Which comparative statistics would you use to establish the superiority of one of the cellular carriers over the others?

4. Make the case for one of the cellular carriers based on criteria of interest to a micro-demographic. Use a criteria other than price.

15

System Normalization

In comparing systems we must derive comparisons that would be considered fair, using the same criteria for competing systems. The principles of normalization apply to systems just as they do at the product and service level. At the same time the system must be implemented per manufacturer's recommendations so as to avoid any suggestion of bias.

Choosing A Reference

Fortunately the output of the system can be normalized rather than attempt to apply the product and service normalizations in some type of summary fashion. System normalization may then be quite simple. For example if we create a system comparison for a coatings system for painting automobiles we might do so using a metric of a Standard Automobile characteristic of the type of automobiles commonly painted. Choose a reference and apply it consistently across competitors for every value proposition for which it is appropriate. Use dimensions and UOMs that are realistic for the use cases to which the metrics are being applied. A coatings system might use a coating UOM of square feet or 100 square feet.

Factorization

As with product and service normalization we apply a factor to arrive at the standard unit. If the system constituents vary in their usage quantities in terms of the standard unit, the factors must be derived and applied at the product or service level before being rolled up into the system level metric. For instance, a coating system comprised of a primer, color coat, and top coat has coverage of 50, 100, and 200 square feet per quart, respectively. This yields factors of 2, 1, and 0.5 to be arrive at system UOM of 100 square feet.

Case Study: Sparkling Pools

In order to compare systems between competitors the PCI team decided to standardize measurements using a pool size of 10,000 gallons. The annual cost for treatment could then be compared consistently across competitors. The plastic pollution statistics for competitors may also be calculated using the standard pool size.

Exercise

1. Using the coatings system example in this chapter and a system UOM of 100 square feet, what is the productivity of the system for a painter who can apply 200 square feet of primer, 50 square feet of color, and 75 square feet of top coat per hour? State productivity in system UOM per hour.

2. If primer is $75 per quart, color is $125 per quart, and top coat is $115 per quart, what is the cost of the system per 100 square feet?

3. A painter is paid $37 per hour. What is the total cost of the system including labor? Assume zero dry time, clean up time, and setup time.

16

Creating An Analysis

The basis of all Product Competitive Intelligence is the analysis of the competitive, product, and micro-demographics intelligence which has been accumulated. Once the data has been acquired it must be transformed into a format which makes it usable for analytical purposes. The analyst can then commence in finding the relationships and statistics of interest.

Competitive Intelligence Data (CID)

CID comprises all of the intelligence acquired regarding competitors, including their capabilities, risk exposures, and other factors that may be useful for positioning your company within the micro-demographics of interest. A swimming pool maintenance company would acquire data on the competing maintenance companies and freelancers in the locale, government data on swimming pool permits, complaints and lawsuits referencing competitors, as well as geospatial data to provide understanding of the logistics challenges facing each competitor.

Product Intelligence Data (PID)

PID is the accumulated information on your products and services as well as those of your competitors. Research on issues with your and your competitors' products, consumers needs and wants, information on recent patent and trademark filings, comparative statistics between your and your competitor products, data on macro and micro trends that may influence the market for your products, will all be useful for analysis.

A swimming pool maintenance company acquiring PID would want to catalog the service and product pricing structure of each competitor, knowledge in depth of the services offered including a common list of attributes across competitors. An assessment of the PID might also yield derivative statistics on the possible profitability of each service offering based on expected time to perform tasks, average commute time, and similar metrics.

Micro-Demographics Intelligence Data (MDID)

MDID consists of the data acquired researching the populations comprising the target markets of the products and services relevant to the analysis. Product intelligence may yield a set of customers who form the basis of this research. For instance, a swimming pool maintenance company may find likely customers to include homeowners with pools and spas, hotels, fitness facilities, and public recreation departments in the surrounding communities. MDID may uncover local organizations to which managers of local hotels may be members, thus providing networking and targeted advertising opportunities. Additional MDID may yield neighborhood association forums where the company might begin to build relationships, discover issues of interest as well as marketing opportunities.

ETL and Cleaning Data

ETL stands for Extract, Transform, and Load. This is the process of moving the data that you are collecting from various sources into a single repository. All data acquisition is subject to errors, so some data cleansing is often necessary. Data is sometimes missing. Depending on the type of data and how the data is stored when loaded, data cleaning may imply differentiating missing data from data having a zero or other default value. In database terms a missing value in a numeric field might be set to NULL.

Extract in ETL is the process of extracting the data from the source documents. Source documents can include a wide variety of types, from paper documents to online databases and web pages. For paper based documents you may find that a fast data entry person is going to be the most efficient means of extracting your data. For online or other digital data sources, a specialist who writes data extraction scripts can help you quickly set up processes for finding and extracting data, as well as transforming that data after acquisition.

Transform in ETL is the process of translating the data into formats and values that are consistent and usable in comparisons. Transformations might include text analysis that derives some type of quantitative measure such as a category, number, or boolean value. Transformation may also be used to conform comparative data into consistent units of measure. When performing transformations it is always a good idea to retain the source data in the event there is a need to change the transformation methods or if there is a question as to the validity of the transformation algorithm.

Loading data involves insertion of transformed data into a repository such as a database or spreadsheet. Although spreadsheets tend to be the default data store for many, they make a poor choice for a number of reasons. A better approach is to use a database and incorporate the ability to move the data into a spreadsheet for analysis. Specialized databases exist which permit some analysis that is difficult to perform in other software. Graph databases such as Neo4J permit analysis of relationships in data. Using a database also makes it easier to use data in non-spreadsheet applications such as AI systems.

Loading implies some type of data structure in most cases. At the early stages of your analysis process it would be in your best interest to consult with a data analyst to determine the data fields, data types, and infrastructure requirements that would best serve your needs. With virtualization and availability of high quality free and Open-Source software, these do not have to be expensive implementations. Poorly implemented systems can be expensive to correct. Do it right the first time.

Analysis

Analysis is based on comparable properties, features, benefits, and any other criteria you can establish in a factual way. Take a holistic approach that looks at the competitive, product, and micro-demographic information in total and in relation to each other. Look for the derivative and summary statistics implied by the data you have accumulated. Examine the data relationships in terms of the trigger points that you have identified through your product and micro-demographic intelligence gathering. For instance, you may determine the labor capacity of your competitors, the services that they offer, and the prices they charge. You may gain an understanding of the limitations associated with their location and geographic distribution of swimming pools in the locale. Knowledge of the chemistry they use servicing pools may be useful for targeting certain types of customers such as those with allergen sensitivity. From this somewhat global understanding of your competitors, their products and services, and your micro-demographics, you are better prepared to derive the comparative statistics that will back up your superiority metrics in support of your value propositions.

Reporting

Reports provide a formal and intelligible means of presenting your analytical results. In many cases an analysis results in tables of numbers which may be difficult to grasp. Translating this information into a textual description, infographics, and summarizations is useful in two ways. First, it provides you with a better understanding of your data and data relationships. Second, the text from reports is probably the same text you will use in your marketing materials, with minor changes.

Using Analytical Results

The point of this work is to arrive at the superiority metrics that are backed by the facts that you have determined through your research and analysis. Claims should be documented by recording the source of the data and the method you used to arrive at the claim. Then if there is any counterclaim or dispute, you can refer directly to your documentation in order to recall how you arrived at your conclusions.

The PCI team was diligent in its collection of competitive, product, and micro-demographics intelligence data. The data was cleaned and imported into the data repository, normalized using the conversion factors that were determined to be useful for consistent comparison across competitors. The micro-demographics data showed that the environmental concerns of some customers could be leveraged in a product redesign that reduced plastic packaging. The analysis of competitor and pool owner geographical data was used in creation of a marketing plan that focused on customers who were ideally located for optimal routing of maintenance crews.

Exercise

1. Pick a product to use for analysis. Make a list of the sources you would use for acquiring competitive, product, and micro-demographics intelligence.

2. Of the sources named in 1, divide them up in terms of data types: print, data, binary

3. Create a plan for extracting or transcribing the data from the various sources.

4. Of the data from the various data sources, which data will need to be transformed and/or normalized after it is extracted? What algorithms would you use?

5. Create a report template to use for presenting your analysis.

17

Creating the System Comparison

In order to compare systems we need to understand to purpose of the system, its objectives, the criteria for success in achieving the objectives, and the implications of achieving or failing to achieve the objective.

Use Cases

The objective of the system we commonly refer to as a *use case*. The usual way we describe a use case is that one or more Actors perform Actions to achieve a Goal. In order to formulate a use case for a system for purposes of comparison between vendors we can document how the Actors specific to each vendor implementation perform required Actions to achieve the Goal. It is possible and normal for the same Actions to be performed by the same Actors for all vendors, but there can be exceptions. For instance, one vendor might provide a product in the system that is ready to use while another might require that the product be mixed or prepared in some way. Another vendor might leave an Action out because the system doesn't require it.

Process Analysis

For each vendor's version of the system, follow the vendor instructions pertaining to the steps required. Everything associated with the system and execution of steps is potential material for comparison, so document everything. If there is an instruction to mix components using a chemical hood, then that should be noted. Document time, effort, expertise, required tools, time between steps in a process, physical requirements and other such statistics that may be useful in comparison. Qualitative claims such as "easy to use" can be analyzed in the light of such detailed information.

Deriving Comparative Metrics

Upon completion of the documentation you should have a list of candidate system metrics that can be compared. The next step is to derive the comparison metrics for the entire system across all competitors. This implies a type of normalization or abstraction. The question is, what do you measure that applies to all versions of the system when each version potentially has some different characteristics. One might summarize as (1) number of steps, (2) total time required, (3) special tools required, and similar generalizations.

During system analysis it is important to note observations such as documentation that is poorly written or badly translated, incorrect or missing instructions, and complicated processes (when an outlier), all of which point to an unpleasant choice for a potential consumer.

Case Study: Sparkling Pools

The PCI team analyzed the use cases associated with pool, spa, and hot tub ownership. The typical use case for all three types was day to day maintenance of the pool chemistry, keeping the pH in the right range, and preventing bacterial and algae growth. There were also special use cases including the initial setup of the maintenance system and dealing with extreme cases such as algae in insufficiently maintained pools.

The team created system comparisons for all of the use cases across all competitors, applying the manufacturers' recommended procedures to the standard 10,000 gallon pool used for comparison. Observations and calculations were made to assess both the qualitative and quantitative differences in the systems.

Exercise

1. Create a use case describing the system objective for a product or service. What are the metrics of success for the use case?

2. Follow the instructions for at least two competitors who offer the product or service described in 1. Document the steps, time requirement, special tools needed, and any other generalizations that you can derive from the comparison.

3. Catalog the metrics that will be compared between products or services.

4. Derive comparison metrics for the entire system across all competitors.

18

Interpreting the Results

Whether we are analyzing at the product and service level or the system level, interpretation of results should be driven by the value propositions defined by the set of micro-demographics and the corresponding positive and negative triggers that have been identified. What are the key facts relevant to each value proposition? Can the facts that we have discovered through our analysis be interpreted in support of any of the value propositions?

Hierarchical Value Propositions

Value propositions for the micro-demographics of interest may have general appeal, meaning they are of interest to nearly everyone, or limited appeal primarily of interest to the micro-demographic in question. It may help to arrange value propositions in a hierarchy similar to an organization chart. Place the most generally applicable value propositions at the top and more specific as you move down the chart. Hierarchies like this can become complex, so expect to repeat some value propositions in the lower levels.

Interpretation Versus Presentation

There is a distinction between the interpretation of results and use of the interpretation. For instance, if the interpretation is that a pound of plastic waste is generated in executing the use case using one vendor's products, that information can be used by scaling it to a large number of users, looking at the use over a long time period, and similar methods in order to amplify the importance of the statistic.

Exercise

1. Select a product at random. What are the competing brands for the product? Analyze the dimensions associated with the product among two or three competitors.

2. For the analytical results in 1, what types of positive or negative triggers appear obvious? Which value propositions might you invoke via your analysis?

3. Pick a value proposition based on the environment. Which interpretations of your analysis can be used to support this value proposition for these products?

19

Use of Results

At the completion of the PCI process we have interpreted the findings of our analysis that derived from competitive intelligence, product intelligence, comparative analysis of products, services, and systems. We have assessed the relevance of our findings with respect to the value propositions important to our target micro-demographics. It is now time to utilize these results in our marketing. We can do this by segmenting the results by customer value areas, develop strategies for deploying information where it will be most effective, utilize media and other resources appropriate for the message to be delivered, utilize creative marketing techniques, and apply superiority marketing strategies.

When segmenting results by customer value proposition some overlap is expected. Most people have multiple areas of concern and goals that they want met. Repetition is good, so delivering the same message to the same person in different venues is a good thing. Create strong, compelling messages. Graphics are effective. Demonstrate the impact of a choice of your product that reinforces your message.

Develop strategies for deploying information in a way that will be most effective. This includes delivering information to your target micro-demographic through multiple exposures. One example we gave was to use a social media influencer to deliver the information. Another might be to use a person active in a forum frequented by members of the micro-demographic. A third would be consulting the members directly in the forum by asking for validation of your planned approach to doing things in your product development that alleviate their concerns. Be extra careful how you handle this. Although marketing is your goal, you must not appear to be marketing or hawking your products or company. Ask the forum owner if it would be OK. Forum members tend to be very sensitive to anything that reeks of spam and will flag your question for removal. Be a participant on the forums where you intend to get your message out. Ask questions and provide answers when you know the answer. Don't argue with people, it's too easy to be pulled into a pointless argument by a troll.

Use Social Media

Use the appropriate resources to spread your message to the relevant social media channels. Choose social media influencers carefully. Look for those who are well regarded, not just those who have followers. There are many potential online and social media venues including special interest groups, zines and similar publications, articles, press releases, Twitter, YouTube, Facebook, and Instagram.

Leverage Special Interests

Special interest groups can be very effective in promoting your products. Although members abhor spam, they love talking about products and constantly argue about features and issues with products, which also make them an excellent resource for finding positive and negative triggers. How do you use a special interest group to promote your product? First, make sure the group isn't controlled by a competitor. It's easy for a competitor to set up a group on Facebook and then control what's posted there, all the while displaying ads that look like official messages. Once you have found some candidate groups, go ahead and sign up as a member. Participate in the group. If someone asks a question that you know the answer to, go ahead and answer it, so long as you can do so without spamming the group. Don't make the answer about your company or products. Next, seek answers to the questions you have about your product's plans and how that correlates with your target market's interests. For instance, you are developing a car wax using pure carnauba wax. You might ask a question like: My company is considering development of new car wax formula. Do people still prefer the results from a carnauba wax or have people moved on to synthetics like polymer coatings? Questions like this on special interest groups can really bring out the zealots. In a way this might be interpreted as a troll, but you've put it out there that you can be persuaded. Let the pro-carnauba forces sway you. Find out what they don't like in currently available carnauba formulas. Perhaps there is a lack of a system that you can provide, such as a pre-wax treatment, applicators, and polishing materials. Perhaps there are certain impurities in carnauba wax for which you have a process to remove.

Zines

Zines are special interest electronic magazines. Magazines have had a tough time surviving in the age of the Internet. Some have moved online, but most of the zines have always been online versions. They still fight for survival. They also need quality content. This makes them an ideal advertising platform. Past issues remain online so your advertising can be visible for years. You can write content that supports the use of your products. You may be able to find a zine for nearly any micro-demographic in which you intend to market your products.

Articles written by you or by influencers on blogs are another effective marketing tool. These are more effective than ads since they are in content that is being consumed rather than the flashing sidebar that is being ignored, and they stay online possibly for years.

Press Releases

A press release is news that is worthy of publication that is distributed to news outlets. The key here is distribution. When marketing into niche demographics the message in the press release needs to be carefully crafted to appeal to the editors of publishers whose focus is that niche. The ideal press release would deliver long awaited news or a significant development that affects the niche.

Twitter

Twitter is a mystery to many, but it can be used to deliver short bursts of news of interest to niche demographics, links to blog posts, references to articles, and similar traffic generating activity. The key to Twitter is following. You need to be both a follower and also follow those in the demographics you intend to pursue. You can't read everything posted, so don't try.

YouTube

YouTube can be a real boon for your product sales. A very effective use of YouTube is posting instructional videos demonstrating the use of your products. People like video over written instructions. In the process of delivering these instructions, it's easy to drop reference to certain superiority metrics without even having to mention a competitor. For instance, if your superiority metric is low or no plastic waste, just mention that as a side benefit of using your product. "Ours is the only product in the industry that produces no plastic waste."

Facebook

Facebook can be an effective marketing venue for some products and services, and the Group functionality can be useful in targeting your niche interests as well as developing a niche group interested in your products. Be careful with the latter. Censorship isn't well received, so make sure that the conditions of membership in the group limit the activity to the type of participation you expect to occur. Don't hesitate to ban bullies and trolls from the groups you control. If your company does business in a local area, then consider making the group's focus that area. For instance, if you are a videographer in Boise then your group could be Boise Videographers. You can place a pinned message in the group to deliver information about your business to those looking for a videographer in Boise, and not incur advertising expenses in the process.

Alternative Marketing

There are many unique and creative approaches you can take to marketing your business. The Guerilla Marketing series of books is a treasure trove of these techniques. Even when you don't apply the actual methods you will start coming up with your own ideas after reading one or two of the books in the series. There is no shortage of stories of creative marketing, such as people planted in lines at Starbucks talking about a newly released product.

Superiority Marketing

Superiority marketing positions your products above your competitors using criteria that is important to the micro-demographic you are addressing. Focus your marketing on delivering the message about these dimensions of superiority. All of the marketing efforts we have outlined are ultimately about delivering these positive and negative triggers where they will have the most impact. Why talk about price when the overriding concern is the environment?

Service Positioning

Positioning a service is similar to positioning a product, but it is the characteristics of the service that are measured. This can be difficult for some services if the quality of the work might only be accurately revealed by a large number of reviews. Bringing to light the way an offered service should be differentiated by promoting those characteristics as if they are missing from competing services is a common tactic. Doing so in a way that targets a specific demographic may be a new approach. For instance, a yard service might use all battery powered equipment and claim to be the only true green yard service. Extra points for solar powered battery chargers.

Case Study: Sparkling Pools

At the end of its intelligence gathering and analysis the PCI team had a rich set of facts about the consumers of its products and services, its competitors, and competing products and services. They were now ready to implement their marketing strategy. One finding of their analysis was that efficiencies could be gained by focusing the marketing efforts for the maintenance business in a small area where most of the pool, spa, and hot tub owners reside. These were most easily targeted with a large four color direct mail post card that promotes the sustainability initiative, premium product line, and lower cost of ownership using their system.

The company invested a small amount sponsoring teams involved in water sports. Banners were printed to be displayed at team events. The expectation was the small amount of equipment sales would approximately offset the cost and they would gain the advertising exposure at the events.

The company put a distinct phone number and web-site URL on the vehicle advertising that permitted them to track the sales associated with the vehicle ads.

Online sales were another marketing target. The marketing team dripped news of the progress on the conversion of their plastic packaging to non-plastic on the news groups where they originally asked for help. This received very positive feedback.

The company hired a mobile application developer to build a troubleshooting application for pool, spa, and hot tub owners. The application was given away but had in-app purchasing that allowed customers to order the suggested chemicals directly from the company.

The company developed a pool technician certification program and implemented it as online training. This provided an additional income stream and allowed those interested in becoming pool technicians to learn the ropes no matter where they lived.

The company reached out to the freelance pool technicians in the area and offered them discounted rates on supplies. They made the certification process part of the requirements for receiving a premium listing on the company website. The program was enthusiastically received by the freelance pool maintenance technicians since it offered an extra degree of credibility and an additional source of leads.

Exercise

1. Create a comprehensive marketing plan incorporating multiple social media channels, special interest groups, YouTube, and Facebook. Utilize the value propositions that you think will be most effective for delivery of your marketing into the selected micro-demographics.

20

System Comparisons

In all but the most basic product and service marketing the most important comparisons are going to be based on systems. A system exists any time that products are sold to be used together or with services. A swimming pool maintenance company might include products as part of its pool maintenance service. A paint manufacturer might sell a coatings system for painting cars. Examining and comparing systems is a powerful approach to multi-product sales.

System Synergy

The system is greater than the sum of its parts. At the most basic level you can certainly compare the constituents individually, and it is a good idea to do that in order to understand the properties and limitations of those components. However it is the synergy derived from the system components used in concert that may prove the superiority of one system over another. Imagine you have a paint shop and paint cars. You are looking at two vendors for paint. One is clearly more expensive than the other. The quality of both is equal. What do you do? On the surface based on the price it appears the best system is the lower priced one, however what if the productivity is much higher using the more expensive system? The key question would be whether your shop would be able to take advantage of the higher productivity and if the productivity gain would produce profits greater than the difference in the price of the two systems.

As we have seen by these examples there are substantial opportunities for differentiation outside the scope of product level comparisons by adopting a systems based approach. Products and services alone may possess many dimensions to compare. Systems potentially add many more. Systems also act to aggregate or summarize the dimensions of their constituents. For instance productivity of a coatings system uses contributing dimensions such as application times, dry times, and similar metrics in order to ascertain a total productivity. Likewise there may be a cost per use calculation that uses the individual product and service features and attributes to derive a metric for cost of use of the system.

There is power in systems. Individual products may fail to impress those trying to solve a problem. They may ignore the system view of the solution by focusing more on the individual components. If you produce a set of products or services comprising a system it would be to your benefit to take a serious look at your system in comparison to those of your competitors.

System Comparison Strategy

How do we approach a system comparison? What is the objective of the system, as opposed to the objectives of the system components? What metrics are used in judging the successful outcome of the system's utilization? How do we analyze these metrics across competing vendors? These are questions that need answers in order to perform a useful comparison. There may be qualitative and quantitative metrics. As we described at the product level, the best qualitative metrics have underlying quantitative metrics that can be used as the basis for a qualitative superiority claim. "Easiest to use" is a qualitative metric that might be supported by an analysis of the total labor requirements.

System dimension may reflect the dimensions of constituents, sums of dimensions, and will possess additional dimensions which may be more abstract or qualitative. Formulate the dimensions that are relevant to the successful outcome of the system objectives.

Using System UOMs

System dimensions have associated UOMs similar to products and services. In comparing dimensions across competitors, normalize these dimensions so that they can be compared in like quantities. Using a consistent type of objective across comparisons aids clarity. For instance, in comparing coating systems we might define something called a Standard Automobile with properties such as paintable surface area. Competing systems might be compared by stating the number of such units that can be painted for a quantity of materials, labor requirement, and total time per unit. If the properties of the Standard Automobile accurately reflect the average automobile painted by a typical shop, then the shop owners can assess the potential profitability increase associated with your system.

The ultimate goal in these comparisons is delivering a message that appeals to the consumer's values. Therefore the comparisons should be derived from the set of value propositions that you intend to address.

Case Study: Sparkling Pools

The PCI team began to see the benefit in a systems comparison approach when it started comparing the total cost of pool ownership using competing systems and found that the Sparkling Pools brand offered the lowest annual cost of ownership. They were also able to make the claim that theirs was the easiest to use system after the repackaging of their chemistry to single use packs. The repackaging also resulted in the lowest plastic waste production of all competitors, making their system the most environmentally friendly.

Exercise

1. Name three systems that you encounter daily. Elaborate on the constituents in each system.

2. Your company has developed a cow feeding system that uses a special feed pellet and feeding machine that you want to sell as a turnkey system that includes delivery of the feed into the feed hopper connected to the machine. Develop a system comparison that shows the superiority of your system to the traditional method of the farmer feeding the cows by hand loading bags of corn into feed stations.

21

Next Steps

Think of PCI as a feedback loop where analysis leads to discovery. The discovery uncovers the opportunities for improvement in your products. For instance, analysis might reveal that you can save money and help the environment by moving to non-plastic packaging, thus increasing the marketability of your product to an environmentally sensitive demographic and increasing per unit revenues in the process. What's not to like?

Continuous Improvement

Continue to identify dimensions of importance to the different segments of your market. Understand your potential and current customers. Look for uses of your products of which you may not be aware. What are the interests of these customers? Why do they have a need or use for the product? If your product deals with an effect, is there a market for a product that prevents the cause? For instance, if your product is being used for treating poison ivy exposure, might there be a market for a product that prevents the exposure?

Use Memetics and the Power of Story

Consider the potential for applying memetics as a marketing strategy. Memetics is a powerful tool and is particularly well suited for marketing new products. Use the power of story to build interest in your effort to develop the product. Seek input from the stakeholders with the most to gain from its successful development. Some products don't have a ready market and customers have to learn about their unmet need. Scarcity can be a powerful motivator. How many times have we seen lines outside Apple stores hoping to be the first to get the newest product release? Build buzz in the communities of interest, using thought leaders to help drive adoption of your product.

Story is an important and impactful form of marketing. People need to relate and when they hear a story they connect with they become interested in learning more. Convincing and interesting stories involve a challenge that is overcome. A hero fights against the odds and comes out on top. You can build an effective story around your efforts to develop your product and the challenges that you had to overcome. The story can unfold in real time, as you interact with and seek input from the communities of interest in your product. As you ask for help and feed the groups updates on your progress interest builds and a meme begins to take hold. The product is beta tested among a small group chosen from those who provided input. Their feedback continues to build interest and spreads the meme. A limited release of the early version creates competition for the first units of production, feeding the meme. Use feedback from the user community to improve the product. Increase availability gradually, keeping demand levels high. Make your customers the rockstars. Feature them on your website using and promoting your products.

Another clever marketing device is to give it away. Place a promotion on your website for a giveaway. Include a marketing permission check box to add interested customers to your email list to receive promotional materials.

Case Study: Sparkling Pools

The PCI team needed a marketing plan for its new premium product line. They wanted to tell the story about the development of the new products, who they were designed for, and then deliver first hand accounts from the consumers of the products. They started the process by asking consumers in targeted news groups about chlorine in pools. They had researched the news groups and knew who the contributors were and what had been said in the past. They referenced a past comment on chlorine as a follow up question to get a conversation started. The respondents noted their problems with chlorine and the marketing team responded that they were working on a solution. They came back a while later saying they had made progress and were looking for participants to test the product in their pools or spas. They had strong interest and selected participants for the market test. The feedback from this group was used to improve the product. Meanwhile the same news groups were asked about their use of aromatherapy products. This led to a second market test and built interest in the aromatherapy products. They now through the multiple meme deployment mechanisms they had used, created much interest in the new products.

Exercise

1. Review your objectives from the exercise in the chapter Introduction.

2. Using your criteria for success, were you able to achieve the objectives you outlined?

3. Consider a specific product, service, or system that you would like to market. How would you create a meme that would target those in a specific special interest group?

Appendix 1

Resources

Books

Gilad, Benjamin - *Business War Games: How Large, Small, and New Companies Can Vastly Improve Their Strategies and Outmaneuver the Competition*, 2008

Gronbach, Kenneth - *Upside: Profiting from the Profound Demographic Shifts Ahead*, 2017

Oriesek, Daniel F.; Schwarz, Jan Oliver - *Business Wargaming: Securing Corporate Value*, 2008

Rijsdijk, Serge A.; Hultink, Erik Jan; Diamantopoulos, Adamantios - *Product intelligence: its conceptualization, measurement and impact on consumer satisfaction*, 2007

Sarkar, Dipanjan - *Text Analytics with Python: A Practical Real-World Approach to Gaining Actionable Insights from your Data*, 2016

Schaeffer, Eric; Sovie, David - *Reinventing the Product: How to Transform your Business and Create Value in the Digital Age*, 2019

Silge, Julia; Robinson, David - *Text Mining with R: A Tidy Approach*, 2017

Tyson, Kirk - *The Complete Guide to Competitive Intelligence (Fifth Edition)*, 2010

Weinstein, Art - *Market Segmentation: Using Demographics, Psychographics and Other Niche Marketing Techniques to Predict and Model Customer Behavior*, 1993

Online Resources

10 Squared Corporation offers consulting in Product Competitive Intelligence, custom software solutions, data gathering, and analysis.
http://10squaredcorp.com/

Academy of Competitive Intelligence offers courses in Competitive Intelligence leading to a certification.
www.academyci.com

Berkeley offers a course in Marketing Analytics through the educational platform EDX.
https://www.edx.org/micromasters/berkeleyx-marketing-analytics

ESRI provides a comprehensive set of Geospatial research tools, maps, and software.
https://www.esri.com/en-us/home

Facebook provides a number of developer tools in its API.
https://developer.facebook.com

Dr. Robert Finkelstein, compiled a comprehensive set of articles on the science of Memetics.
Memetics Compendium
https://robotictechnologyinc.com/images/upload/file/Memetics%20Compendium%205%20February%202009.pdf

Google provides research tools for trend analysis.
https://trends.google.com

Institute for Competitive Intelligence offers instruction in Competitive Intelligence.
www.institute-for-competitive-intelligence.com/

Intel Techniques is a resource for Open Source Intelligence books and software.
https://inteltechniques.com/

Janes offers training in Open Source Intelligence.
www.ihsmarkit.com/products/consulting-open-source-intelligence-training-osint.html

Open Source Intelligence Training offers two day workshops on Open Source Intelligence.
http://opensourceintelligencetraining.org/

SANS offers a course in Open Source Intelligence Gathering and Analysis
https://www.sans.org/ondemand/course/open-source-intelligence-gathering?msc=od-hp

Siemens offers products that support Product Intelligence
www.plm.automation.siemens.com/global/en/products/performance-analytics/product-intelligence.html

Strategic & Competitive Intelligence Professionals is a professional organization for practitioners of Competitive Intelligence. They also provide training.
www.scip.org

Twitter provides an API for reading and creating tweets.
https://developer.twitter.com

Wharton Online offers training in business analytics through the online education platform Coursera
https://www.coursera.org/specializations/business-analytics

Appendix 2

Memes and Memetics

Definitions

Memetics was mentioned briefly in Chapter 4, Product Competitive Intelligence and elsewhere in the book. This is a further elucidation of the key concepts in memetics. A meme is an idea that spreads through a population like a virus. There are some other definitions put forward in Richard Brodie's excellent book, *Virus of the Mind.* [1]

Dawkins: A meme is a basic unit of cultural transmission, or imitation.

Plotkin: A meme is the unit of cultural heredity analogous to the gene and is the internal representation of knowledge.

Dennett: A meme is a kind of complex idea that forms itself into a distinct memorable unit. It is spread by vehicles that are the physical manifestations of the meme.

Brodie: A meme is a unit of information in a mind whose existence influences events such that more copies of itself get created in other minds.

That last definition is starting to sound more like a virus, isn't it? Memetics is the science of memes, how they infect populations, and how they spread.

Meme has become itself a type of meme in popular culture in that it represents images, videos, and animated gifs that are used in response to current events. A common meme in this context is a photograph of a couple who have walked past an attractive female. The male has turned around to look at the female and his partner is looking at him with disdain. The photo is captioned in some way that makes fun of the current event.

1   Brodie, Richard - *Virus of the Mind*, 1996

Mechanisms of Proliferation

As Brodie describes it, memes spread through three mechanisms. The first is through conditioning, through the repetition of the idea over and over again. How many ad jingles do you remember because you have heard them so many times? The second mechanism is cognitive dissonance, when the mind tries to make sense out of something unfamiliar. Unexpected behavior may lead to an attempt to make sense of the behavior. The third, and probably most powerful mechanism, leverages things you care about or that naturally attract your attention.

An effective use of memes in marketing is the creation of a need in the target audience.

need - require (something) because it is essential or very important.

How Red Camera Dominated Its Market

A most excellent example of memes in marketing involved the creation and marketing of the Red Cinema Camera. In the early days of digital cinematography filmmakers were limited by the small sensor size of the available cameras. Typical affordable cameras had 1/3" sensors. More expensive cameras used by news organizations had 2/3" sensors. Even the larger sensor cameras lacked the visual aesthetic associated with motion picture film having a much larger area. To compensate, filmmakers employed some innovative approaches such as using the small sensor camera to film an image projected onto a spinning ground glass by a lens from a larger format camera. This all changed with the introduction of the Canon 5D, a still camera with a 35mm sensor which had a video mode. The video mode was added as a feature for photojournalists to shoot short video in the field, however it was seized on by filmmakers and an industry formed around the tools and accessories needed to make the 5D an effective cinema camera.

Shortly after the introduction of the 5D several camera makers began producing still cameras with video modes as well as a few video cameras with larger sensors. However these cameras all had various shortcomings and the filmmakers' quest for the perfect large sensor video camera continued. Then the Red Camera rumors started. Word came out that the inventor of Oakley sunglasses had decided to build a large sensor cinema camera that would meet all the desires of these filmmakers. Information on progress was dripped in filmmaking forums. The meme was building. The company was developing a rabid following. The company promised "4k for $4k", a reference to the dream camera's resolution and price. After many delays, changes in the camera's specifications, and the realization that the price of a working camera would be nowhere near the target, the believers still believed and the company is now one of the major producers of digital cinema cameras.

Red used all three mechanisms in proliferation of its meme. The continuous dripping of news conditioned those interested in the camera. "4K for $4K" is a cognitive disconnect with the expectation of prices in the tens of thousands of dollars. Lastly, the camera was designed to appeal to the areas of great concern such as camera resolution and the visual aesthetic holy grail.

Memes are effective in marketing. There is much more to memetics than we can cover in this book and a great start if you would like to learn more is Brodie's book. Another good source of information is the Memetics Compendium compiled by Dr. Robert Finkelstein.[2]

2 https://robotictechnologyinc.com/images/upload/file/Memetics%20Compendium%205%20February%2009.pdf

Exercise

1. How many memes in current culture can you identify?

2. Think of how you could use a meme to market your product or service. Which mechanism or mechanisms would you employ? How would you build interest using the meme?

Made in the USA
Columbia, SC
15 January 2021